SON OF BUM

SON OF BUM

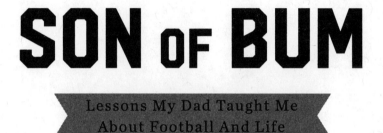

Lessons My Dad Taught Me
About Football And Life

WADE PHILLIPS

with **VIC CARUCCI**

DIVERSIONBOOKS

Diversion Books
A Division of Diversion Publishing Corp.
443 Park Avenue South, Suite 1008
New York, New York 10016
www.DiversionBooks.com

Cover photo: Sam C. Pierson Jr. © Houston Chronicle. Used with permission.
Back cover photo: Jeff Lewis, courtesy of LA Rams.

Image credits: page 137 by Amy Headington/Images of Grace Photography; pages
5, 170, 194, and 206 by Bart Bragg; page 203 property of Eric Bakke; page 151
property of Wyatt McSpadden; page 130 property of San Diego Chargers. All other
photos from the author's personal collection.

Quotations from *He Ain't No Bum*, by O. A. "Bum" Phillips and Ray Buck, are
marked with an asterisk (*). Used with permission.

For more information, email info@diversionbooks.com

First Diversion Books edition May 2017
Print ISBN: 978-1-68230-808-0
eBook ISBN: 978-1-68230-807-3

To my wonderful wife and best friend, Laurie, who has stood beside me through forty-eight football years; to my daughter, Tracy, and son, Wesley, who have been the best children a parent could ask for; to my friend, Vic, the talented writer who spent countless hours making this my story; to my friend and agent, Gary, who encouraged me to do this project to tell the story of Dad and me. Most of all, to my dad, for being the kind of man who made me want to tell about our relationship and my love for him. And love you, Mom, for raising me right.

—Wade Phillips

To Rhonda, who gave me Kristen and Lindsay, who married Larry and Ryan, who have been two incredible sons to this bum; to my four-legged Coach, who spent countless hours curled up in his usual spot on the green chair as I tapped away on my keyboard. Miss you, buddy!

—Vic Carucci

CONTENTS

CHAPTER ONE

BABY DERBY

"There are four things in life I know somethin'
about: pickup trucks, gumbo, cold beer
and barbecued ribs."

—Bum Phillips
from *He Ain't No Bum*

Friday night is normally date night for my wife Laurie and me. But it wasn't going to be any normal Friday night on October 18, 2013.

I was the defensive coordinator for the Houston Texans, and we were getting ready to play the Chiefs in Kansas City. The Friday before a Sunday game is an early day for everyone on an NFL team, because most of the preparation is done by Thursday night. On Friday, you practice in the morning and you have the afternoon off.

The time allows coaches and players to get caught up on stuff they haven't been able to do all week with a schedule that has everyone coming in early in the morning and going home at night, sometimes late depending on when you're putting together the game plan and your meeting schedule. Friday afternoons during the season are good for running errands, maybe getting a haircut.

My plan after leaving work that day was to get in the car

At Super Bowl 50 with (BACK ROW L-R) my brother-in-law, Mark England; my sister, Kim England; Aurelien Bonzon; my daughter-in-law, Anna Phillips; David Fish; my son, Wes; Jack McCarthy; and Buddy Hagner; (FRONT ROW L-R) Nancy Agawa; Trish Hagner; my sister, Andrea McCarthy; my wife, Laurie and me; my sister, Susan Phillips; my sister, Deedean Hurta; Dicke Hurta; and Buddy Hagner; and (KNEELING L-R) Malcolm Agawa and my daughter, Tracy Phillips. NOT PRESENT: my sister, Cicely Devore.

and drive two hours to Goliad, Texas, where my father, Bum Phillips, lived. Bum was a coaching legend in Texas, first at the high school level and then in the NFL. He was one of the most beloved men in the business, a giant figure who did things to revolutionize the way the game is played and especially the way it's coached. He left his mark all over the league, but none bigger than the one he left on me.

At the time, I wasn't thinking about Bum Phillips, the legend. I was just thinking about Bum Phillips, my dad. He was dying and I had to be with him.

His health had taken a bad turn earlier that fall and he was getting hospice care at his home, which was a ranch. He had always dealt with asthma and lung problems. They were things he had lived with for a long time, and as he got older, they started catching up with him. A month earlier, right around the time of his ninetieth birthday, he sat down with two of my sisters and Laurie and me, and told us that he had lived a good life, that he felt good about everything he had done and about all of us.

"I have a great family," Daddy said. "I'm not giving up, but I know I'm in bad health."

That was hard for me to hear. I cried, along with everyone else sitting around him.

He was just lying in the bed when I got there on Friday. He really didn't acknowledge anyone or anything. I just kind of held his hand. He looked peaceful.

I stayed for a while and nothing really changed. I told him I loved him, then I got back in the car and drove two hours back home on Interstate 10 to Houston.

That night, the two Texas high schools where Daddy coached were playing each other, Port Neches-Groves and Nederland. These are neighboring towns; you can't tell where

With the Bum Phillips Bowl Trophy, presented to the winner of the Port Neches-Groves/ Nederland game. Bum coached both teams, and they form one of the biggest high-school football rivalries in Texas.

one ends and the other begins. Bum Phillips Way runs from Port Neches through Nederland, so it was a huge rivalry, dating all the way back to 1925. When Bum was at Nederland, he beat Port Neches-Groves every year. Then Port Neches-Groves hired him to beat Nederland, and he did. Today their game is called the Bum Phillips Bowl, and there's a giant trophy that goes to the winner.

When I got home, I logged onto the Internet to listen to the game. At halftime, the score was tied.

That's when I got the call from Debbie, my father's wife of twenty-three years, telling me that Dad had died. I thought it was kind of ironic, the two teams he'd coached being in a tie at that very moment, as if paying tribute to him. I got back in the car and headed back to Goliad.

There were so many thoughts going through my mind. I felt sad, of course, but at the same time, I was happy that my dad had been the man that he was. Not just because of what he meant to football, but also because he was uniquely himself. You can't be that guy anymore in the NFL. You can't be a guy wearing a cowboy hat on the sideline...unless it has a Nike swoosh on it. You can't wear cowboy boots on the sideline. You can't say what's really on your mind.

It was just a different time in the 1970s and '80s when Dad coached the Houston Oilers and then the New Orleans Saints. Now you've got to be a guy that can answer all of the questions from the media in a certain way. You've got to say all the right things instead of what you want to say. You can't be the good ol' boy that he was. You can't be yourself.

Money has changed everything. I'm not talking about the millions that players get paid. I'm happy to see them make as much as they can. They deserve it, because they're the lifeblood of the NFL. Fans watch the game because of them.

I'm talking about the billions that the league makes from television and sponsorships and merchandise. With all of that money the owners take in, they have all kinds of rules and restrictions for everyone involved. They want you to look a certain way and act a certain way. It's actually a part of your contract. You have to wear the gear they assign you to wear, because you're a walking commercial. The NFL wants fans to see the clothes you have on so they'll buy them.

None of that was going on when my dad was coaching. He wasn't trying to sell anything. He was just a coach.

He loved his football team. He loved his players. He didn't mind telling them that, either.

Daddy was pretty funny. He could always say things in his own way that made you laugh. I accused him of having someone writing that stuff for him, but it all just came off the top of his head. That was the way he was all the time.

I don't know where it came from. He always said his dad was a pretty funny guy, but I never did get to know my grandfather well because I was just a kid when he died. My only memory of him was when he was on oxygen and would pull off the mask to smoke a cigarette, then take the oxygen again. All I can remember thinking was, *This is not good. You shouldn't be doing that.*

When I got back to Goliad, Debbie told me something about those final moments I got to spend with Daddy that I'll never forget.

"You know he waited for you before he died, don't you?" she asked.

• • •

My dad was my hero. Pretty much everything I know about life, football, and coaching, I learned from him.

He shaped me as a man, as a husband, as a father, and as a football coach. It was a nonstop education that first played out in the field house at Nederland High School, where he held his first coaching job. I always came by to visit, from when I was seven years old. That education continued all the way through the time we coached together in college and the NFL, and even after he retired.

Dad's actual name was Oail Andrew Phillips. There are a couple of different stories about how he became known as Bum. I'm going to set the record straight by telling the real one. For one thing, he needed a nickname, because no one could pronounce Oail, which sounds like "Uhl." His daddy was Oail Sr., but everybody called him "Flop."

The version Dad liked to tell about the origin of Bum was that when his sister, Edrina, was three, she stammered and when she tried to say "brother" it came out "b-b-b-bum." The real story—and I know this because it came from his mother—was that when he was a little kid, he got into a nest of bumblebees. It was a scary experience that stayed with him.

In the country, they don't say "bumblebees." They say "bummel bees." After that, his mom and dad always would say, "Bummel! Bummel! Bummel!" to try to scare him. Eventually, his mother started calling him Bummel. But Aunt JoAnnette couldn't say it when she was a little kid. She could only say Bum.

Even though the other explanation makes no sense, I think Dad liked telling the story that way because he didn't want to go through the trouble of telling the longer version every time. He also liked to say that one of the best things he ever did for me was not naming me Oail III.

Daddy was a genuine cowboy. He wore a ten-gallon hat and

Hanging out with Daddy, a genuine cowboy.

cowboy boots; my mother claimed the only time she ever saw him wear dress shoes was on their wedding day. He rode horses and chewed tobacco. His granddaddy was a rancher, and that was the life Daddy knew—ranching and football.

He wasn't getting paid a lot when he first started coaching at the high school level, so he would compete in rodeos on the weekend. He was a bulldogger. That's where you jump off the horse, grab a steer by the horns, turn his neck, and take him to the ground. Whoever did it the fastest would win.

In 1947, when I was fixing to be born, Dad was working on the Edgar Brown Ranch in Orange, Texas. The ranch belonged to one of the two richest families in town. The other was the Starks. The Browns and the Starks both had ranches, and they basically owned Orange at that time.

Daddy would always look for ways to earn some extra income working on the ranch. People would pasture their horses there, and there was one time a world-champion quarter horse happened to be on the ranch. In fact, he had just set the world record in the quarter mile.

Back then, there weren't horse-racing tracks everywhere, so people would stage weekend match races where you could bet on your own horse. Dad and one of the other ranch hands decided they would take the champion quarter horse to a match race in Louisiana, just over the Texas border. Dad was going to bet all the money he had on him, which wasn't a lot.

The people running those match races wouldn't hesitate to pull a gun on you and shoot you if they thought you were cheating them. Fearing that someone might recognize the horse's markings, my dad and his friend used brown shoe polish to cover a big white spot on the front of his head. They also told the guy who would be riding him to pull back as much as possible. They didn't want to win by a wide margin and raise suspicions.

The horse won and as soon as he crossed the finish line, Daddy and the other guy ran over and threw blankets on him. They wanted to get him out of there as soon as they could, especially when they noticed that the horse's sweat was making the shoe polish come off. They ran him into the trailer, collected their winnings, and took off.

My dad's share was about $150...just enough to pay the hospital bill when I was born. Nice to know I at least had a sure thing bringing me into the world.

My connection to Dad's ranching experience didn't end there. The name on my birth certificate is Harold Wade Phillips, because Harold and Wade were the names of two of the other ranch hands who worked with Daddy.

• • •

At twenty-nine months old, sharing a moment with my mom, Helen.

It's hard for people outside of Texas to grasp just how big high school football really is there. *Friday Night Lights* isn't just the title of a book or a movie or a TV series. It's a way of life. If you played sports in Texas, you played football. My dad was no exception. He was a really good baseball player at French High School in Beaumont, but he was a big star in football. It just came naturally to him.

For Daddy, playing the game was the easy part. The hard part was convincing his father to let him play. Oail Sr. was a dairyman and a truck driver and did a bunch of other odd jobs. He was dead set against his son playing football because he wanted him to come home after school to do his chores.

He also didn't want him risking a broken leg that would keep him from doing those chores. Daddy went ahead and played anyway, and every day he came home late because of practice, his daddy whipped him. This went on for about a week before his daddy said, "You really do want to play football, don't you, son?"

"Yes sir, I do."

"Okay, make sure you get your chores done when you get back home…and if you get your leg broke, just remember I told you so."

You'd get forty or fifty people showing up just to watch a spring training practice at Port Neches-Groves. During the season, there would be an announcement every Friday morning over the loudspeaker at the elementary school, letting kids know they could buy their game tickets. A huge line would form immediately. Attendance would be around ten thousand to twelve thousand for each game and you needed to buy season tickets if you wanted to sit in the nonstudent section.

Laurie's daddy, a shift worker in an oil refinery, had two of them for Port Neches-Groves. Everyone knew him as Stinky, and when he passed away, people called the house and said, "Hey, we're sorry to hear about Stinky…but are y'all gonna keep your season tickets?" That's Texas high school football right there.

The families of players from Port Neches-Groves and Nederland still work together in the refineries, and the winner of their annual game loves having those bragging rights for the year. Every twelve months, just like clockwork, you have parents, brothers, sisters, uncles, aunts, and cousins either saying, "We beat you!" or "Wait 'til next year!" That's the extent of it. Football is a game. It means a lot for everybody in Texas, but it's not war. It's not life or death. It's just football.

Growing up, high school football got me hooked on the game because there weren't any NFL teams in Texas at the time. The only NFL team we saw on TV was the Chicago Bears, so I became a Bears fan. But I went to all of the Nederland games. I idolized all of those players and the coaches, especially my dad.

One player I really looked up to on that team was Leon Fuller. He was a 160-pound running back and defensive back who went on to play at Tyler Junior College from 1956 to 1958.

In '58 when my dad was the coach at Jacksonville High, "Bear" Bryant, now the coach at Alabama, called to say he was looking for a defensive back.

"I've got this kid in junior college named Leon Fuller," Daddy said.

"Do you think he can play?"

"Yes, sir, I think he can play."

"OK, he's got a scholarship. Just send him to Alabama."

Leon didn't have the money to take the bus from Texas to Tuscaloosa, so my dad paid for his ticket. He wanted to reimburse Daddy with cash, but Daddy got all of the payback he needed when Leon went on to become an all-SEC safety his first year, an all-conference halfback and safety his second year, and captain of the Crimson Tide.

Leon went on to coach football. He was defensive coordinator at Texas for five seasons and head coach at Colorado State for seven. I actually ended up hiring him as my defensive backs coach when I was head coach of the Broncos in 1994.

Daddy told me another story that just reinforces the meaning of Texas high school football. He was working late one night at Nederland when the phone rang in the field house. The call was for Joe Sibley, one of the assistant coaches on the staff. It was his wife.

"Joe, I'm getting tired of this," she said. "You're never home; we never get to go anywhere." She was crying as she went down the list of all the things about his job that were upsetting her. Finally, she said, "You love football more than you love me."

Joe paused for a second. Then he said, "Yeah, but I love you more than basketball."

In 1962, when my dad left a head coaching job at Texas Western (now known as the University of Texas at El Paso) to become head coach at Port Neches-Groves, he actually received a pay raise. He brought three assistant coaches and a trainer with him, and they all got pay raises, too.

When Dad went to work in Port Neches, which was near where he was from, he told our family that it was the last time he was going to be a coach. He was forty years old, and his plan was to eventually leave coaching and become an athletic director until he retired.

Two years later, he got an offer to become defensive coordinator at the University of Houston. Of course, he accepted it. As much as he might have thought that it made sense to spend the rest of his career working close to home, he also knew that there was more he wanted to do coaching-wise and he couldn't pass up that opportunity.

Daddy also said I was going to go to the University of

Making a tackle, and forcing a fumble, as a linebacker at the University of Houston.

Houston, no matter what. He liked to say, "I've told him everything to do his whole life, so I'm going to tell him where to go
to school, too."

When I was playing as a sophomore, he would say something to the entire defense after every play in practice, but I
knew it was meant for me. He'd say, "We need to play quicker,
we need to use our hands better, we need to hustle more, we
need to run to the ball better." I knew "we" meant "me."

I wasn't a great player, but I didn't make many mistakes. I
knew what to do and I knew what other players were doing. I
knew techniques. I had good coaches who taught fundamentals.

My dad helped me to expand my football knowledge by
letting me sit in on meetings with the defensive staff. When
they talked about other players on the team, what they could
and couldn't do, my dad would say to me, "Hey, that doesn't go
out of this room." I wasn't going to betray that trust. It wouldn't
be right, for one thing, and for another, the football education I was getting was too valuable for me to do anything to
screw it up.

By being around coaches all the time in those meetings,
I was able to make up mentally whatever I might have lacked
physically and start for three years at linebacker. I absorbed
things that a lot of other guys probably didn't know. I could find
the football. I could diagnose plays. I knew about formations.
I was good at anticipating what the offense was going to do. I
could see what players were giving away, such as whether the
guard was going to pull or not based on his stance. If he was
really light on his hands while leaning forward, that told me he
was about to pull and I'd be ready for that.

I would watch the tailback to see which way he looked when
he came out of the huddle. Same with the tight ends. A lot of

times, if they're going to block down, meaning they're going to take on the defensive end, they'll look to the inside.

• • •

After two seasons at the University of Houston, Dad got his first NFL coaching job as a defensive line coach for the San Diego Chargers. He told me that Sid Gillman, the Chargers' coach, was looking for a good college coach for the job, and called two of the top coaches in college football—Darrell Royal, of Texas, and Frank Broyles, of Arkansas—for a recommendation. Both said, "Bum Phillips."

Besides building up his football knowledge base, this was another benefit of my dad going to all of those college spring training camps when he was a high school coach. Texas and Arkansas were two of the schools he had visited and he made a good impression on their coaches as well.

The Vietnam War was going on at the time and young men were wearing their hair longer. In that respect, NFL locker rooms didn't look much different than the rest of society. Knowing my dad was an ex-Marine and always wore a crew cut, I asked what he thought about what he was seeing around him.

"I don't worry about all that," he said. "They're the same person whether their hair is long or not."

That was Dad. He didn't judge people by the length of their hair or the color of their skin or the kind of clothes they wore. He would tell me, "Hey, if four of you are in a fox hole and one's got to stay awake while the other three sleep, it doesn't matter what color his skin is, his nationality, or any of that stuff. That guy just has to do his part." That kind of stuck with me.

When the Chargers fired Sid after the 1970 season, my dad ended up as defensive coordinator for Hayden Fry at Southern Methodist University. SMU had the top defense in the Southwest Conference while Dad was there, but even though the Mustangs went 7–4, the coaching staff was fired in 1972. Daddy was looking for work again.

Next stop, Oklahoma State, for another defensive coordinator position.

CHAPTER TWO

COACHING ISN'T BITCHING

"You gotta have rules, but you also gotta allow for
a fella to mess up every once in awhile."

—Bum Phillips
from *He Ain't No Bum*

That's me, in the middle of my dad (left) and the legendary Paul "Bear" Bryant, when they were coaching Texas A&M in the 1957 Gator Bowl.

OF THE MANY QUALITIES I ADMIRED ABOUT MY DAD, THE ONE I admired most was his great common sense. He always seemed to point something out or make a suggestion that would cause everyone around him to say, "Why didn't I think of that?" His real gift was knowing what things to do and when to do them. I like to think I emulate that.

A lot of people think coaching is hollering or screaming at somebody. My dad always said—and I've always said this, too—"Coaching isn't bitching. There's no use bitching about something that's already happened." That's the way a lot of coaches coach. They bitch at guys after the mistake happens, calling them names or whatever, instead of teaching them how to do it right in the first place. The object is to get them to be better players. When you spend more time harping on what they do wrong than showing them how to do it right, you aren't coaching. You're just bitching.

My dad was unlike a lot of coaches in another way: he had no problem with being friends with his players. He believed you shouldn't be afraid to get close to somebody. I don't think there's anything wrong with that, either. Dad was approachable to all his players, and I think that's a big reason why they played hard for him. When players know that you're pulling for them and trying to get them to do their best, that's usually a pretty good combination. I know I'd rather play for somebody I like than somebody I don't like. Common sense, right?

Daddy never believed in using fear as motivation, and he was right about that. These are grown men, and more than a few have seen some of the worst things that life can dish out long before they ever get to the NFL. They're not scared of you. They're not scared of anyone. It's part of the mindset that goes with being a football player. There was a time when coaches could get away with threatening players by saying they would cut them. If you do that now, that player's going to say, "Go ahead and cut me. I'll just play somewhere else."

Using threats and kicking guys in the butt? I just don't think you get the most out of your team that way.

On the flip side of the coin, coaching is about being honest, too. If players make a mistake or they need to hustle more or they need to do things a certain way, you've got to be honest with them about that. You can't just say, "Hey, I want to be your friend and I'm only going to tell you what you want to hear." But there's a difference between that and constantly bitching at them.

Dad warned me early on that there would be a backlash for taking more of a player-friendly approach. "People will say you're too soft because you get along with the players," he said. "But that doesn't matter as long as they respect what you say and do what you say. After that, you just let them do the things that they can do well. You get a good player and a good team that way."

Nice guys can finish first. That's what Daddy always believed. That's what I've always believed. You're not trying to get all the players to like you, because that's not going to happen. But as long as they know you respect them, they seem to reciprocate.

He just had a great feel for how to connect with his players and get the most out of them without trying to jam things down their throats. Daddy never talked about winning and losing. He just talked about playing your best, doing your best, working to be the best—all those things. You never heard him say things like, "Now, we're gonna go out and kick their asses!" Or, "We're better than them!" Or, "If we do this, we're gonna win!" He just talked about being the best you can be in every way possible— being the best team, being a family, being a great teammate.

My dad struggled to find common sense thinking in the Marines. He enlisted in 1941, right after the Japanese attack on Pearl Harbor, and joined the Marines' elite unit. But he quickly discovered that he and the Marines didn't see eye to eye. Daddy said that they sent him to California to march for hundreds of miles before going over to Guadalcanal. That just didn't make sense to him.

"I don't want to march," he said. "I want to go over

and fight. I'm trying to help win this war, and we're over here marching in California."

He never got beyond a buck private, because he kept getting busted for not following orders. He would tell me that his superiors would always say, "Let's go get 'em for the glory of the Marines! We're not gonna wait for the Air Force." My dad's thinking was, *We're going to go for the glory of the Marines by not waiting for Air Force cover...and we're going to get a bunch of guys killed.* He balked at that kind of stuff, especially when the people in command would all stay behind. To them, "we" didn't mean "us." It meant "them."

The first time they took his battalion out on a boat in the South Pacific, they went a long ways to an island where they were told the Japanese they would attack the next day were. My dad didn't see the point in waiting. He got together with a bunch of his guys and said, "We don't need to wait until tomorrow. We came to fight, let's go get 'em now."

They left the boat in the middle of the night. After crossing through the jungle to the other side of the island, they came upon a big bonfire. "We ran in there with our machine guns and stuff...only to find it was a bunch of native pygmies," he told me. "The pygmies started to scatter, running everywhere." He found out later that it was just a practice deal for them, that there weren't really any Japanese on the island.

My dad hit the beach and fought in the war. He saw a bunch of guys around him killed. In fact, so many died, they had to disband their battalion before the war was even over. But my father knew that he and the Marines just weren't meant for each other.

Years later, during a press conference as the Oilers' coach, Dad talked about his decision to join the Marine Corps after high school. He said, "I learned my lesson. I never joined anything else the rest of my life. I went in as a private and, thirty-one months later, I came out as a private. I thought they couldn't win that war without me. Then I got in there and I thought they couldn't win because of me. The Marine Corps was real spit 'n' polish. I wasn't."

After World War II, Daddy went to work in an oil refinery and completed his degree at Lamar Junior College before enrolling at Stephen F. Austin University, where he played two years of football on the way to graduating with a degree in education. In 1954, he took his first coaching job in football as head coach at Nederland. I was seven, and I was the water boy when I wasn't hanging around the field house just so I could be around him.

In those days (and I know how crazy this sounds now, when there's much more concern about safety), players weren't actually allowed to drink water during practice or games because it was considered a sign of weakness. I did carry around a bucket of water, but the players could only dip a towel into the bucket and then put it on their face. A lot of them would also suck the water out of their towels, trying to get as much relief as possible in the intense heat and humidity.

It was at Nederland that Dad came up with one of his all-time best common-sense ideas: a numbering system that told each defensive lineman where to line up and his responsibility in a particular defense. Pretty much every team at every level of football uses it to this day, although with some modifications. I've made some myself, but at the heart of it, you have something that makes so much more sense than the previous method of making guys remember where to line up based on code words, such as "Seven Diamond" or "Tiger" or "Cat" or "Mouse."

Daddy's system simplified the whole process of telling guys where to go and what to do, as well as teaching them the defense, which they could learn much faster through numbers. That was especially helpful at the high school level.

The numbers identify the "technique alignments" for your four or three defensive linemen, depending on the type of front you use. The basic system starts in the middle with zero technique, which means head up on the center, and goes all the way up to nine technique, which is outside the tight end.

For instance, you could call "Twenty-seven/fifteen," and that would mean that on the strong side of the offense, where the tight end is located, you'd have one defensive lineman in two technique (head up on the guard), and the other in seven technique (inside of the tight end), and on the weak side, where there's no tight end, you'd have a defensive lineman in one technique (inside the guard), and another in five technique (outside the tackle).

Daddy was always thirsting for football knowledge. He'd regularly jump into the school car and drive out to watch college spring training drills at the University of Oklahoma and the University of Arkansas. He learned a lot from watching the way Bud Wilkinson ran the Oklahoma Sooners practices, such as dividing everything into segments. Dad would take those ideas and incorporate them into his practices at Nederland.

He rose quickly as a great coach, and everybody in Texas high school football knew who he was. He was piling up regular-season wins and playoff victories. Daddy developed a reputation for being an innovator because of his desire to constantly expand his knowledge of the game by seeing how other coaches did things, and then applying his common-sense view of everything.

Besides the numbering system, he also was one of the few high school coaches at that time teaching "rule blocking" to his offensive linemen. With rule blocking, rather than telling the guard to just hit whoever's in front of him, you say, "You've got over, outside, and linebacker." That means you want him to follow a pattern of first blocking the guy who lines up over him, then the one who lines up outside of him, and then the linebacker who's off the ball. As I said, Daddy might not have talked a lot about Xs and Os, but he knew them cold.

• • •

My parents moved eight times from when I was in kindergarten to when I was in twelfth grade, as Bum bounced from coaching job to coaching job. As a coach's son and a coach, I've moved twenty-two times and lived in eleven states. It wasn't always easy, but as a kid it was the only life I knew so I didn't really see myself as being all that different from everyone else. As a coach, you accept it as part of the job. It's what you sign up for.

When I played high school football, one of the big drawbacks of my father's moves was a rule in Texas that made you lose a year of varsity eligibility when you transferred. It didn't apply to baseball or basketball, only football. That's because rich oil towns such as Abilene would cherry pick all-state sophomores and juniors from other schools by hiring their parents to work for the oil companies. But the rule hurt players like me, who were legitimately transferring. It eventually changed to where—if you could produce a letter explaining your circumstances—you didn't lose a year of eligibility, although that didn't happen until after I graduated.

As a sophomore, when my father became head coach at Texas Western, we moved to El Paso, so I had to play junior varsity. Then, a year later, when my dad became head coach at

Port Neches-Groves, I transferred again as a junior. Again, I was stuck on the JV team. Those back-to-back years of varsity ineligibility didn't bother me because I still got to play. More than anything, I liked to play ball.

By then, everyone had started calling me "Junior Varsity All-America." As someone who should have been starting on varsity, I was way better than the other players on my junior varsity team and the guys we played. Back then, you had to play both ways. As quarterback, I scored two to three touchdowns per game, and just killed people from the middle linebacker position before having my season shortened by a fractured leg.

I suffered the injury while taking a hit and the ambulance drove onto the field and took me to our school's orthopedic surgeon. My dad drove separately and I had an X-ray before he got to the doctor's office. The knee was full of fluid, like three

Before defense ruled my football life, I was a quarterback at Port Neches-Groves High School.

times its normal size, because the fracture was right above my knee in the femur.

"Well, you've torn up everything in your knee," the doctor said. "We're going to have to go in to operate. As soon as your dad gets here, I'll tell him."

When my dad walked in, the surgeon told him his diagnosis and said, "We'll have to take him right now and operate."

"No, you're not, either," my dad said. "I'm going to take him somewhere else for another opinion."

That came as a surprise to the surgeon. I was actually shocked, too, because I just assumed the doctor knew what he was talking about. But Daddy had another doctor, an older one that he knew in Beaumont. Dad told me that he trusted him and wanted him to give my leg a second look before we went ahead with any surgery. My dad gave him a call, they put me back in the ambulance, and we headed for the hospital in Beaumont, which was about thirty minutes away.

After we got there, the second doctor took a look at my leg and said, "Well, Bum, he's got a broken leg, but I don't know if he's got torn ligaments or anything like that."

Unfortunately, the way he was going to find out was to start twisting my leg. "Wade, this is going to hurt," he warned me. "But I need to do this." He was right. It hurt like heck. But after he was done twisting, he turned to my dad and said I didn't have any torn ligaments.

"We'll just put him in a cast for six weeks and he'll be alright," the doctor said.

My dad knew, at that time especially, if the surgeon went in and opened up my knee, I'd have no future in football. I wouldn't be able to play another game in high school or college. Just immobilizing the fracture meant, after it was healed, I could come back to play on the varsity team in my senior year.

The cast ran all the way from my hip down to my foot. I just lay in bed for six weeks. I couldn't even go to school. One day, my dad came into my bedroom with some dumbbells for me to use just so I could do something to build strength while I was on my back. My mother was furious. It was probably as mad as I had ever seen her get at him.

"Leave the poor kid alone!" she yelled. "He's got a broken leg!"

I didn't mind. I was so bored that at least it gave me something to do. I pretty much just lifted weights in bed and watched TV. After six weeks, I got a walking cast and went to school on crutches. Once I got out of that cast and I could walk without crutches, my dad said, "Alright, after school every day, you walk around the track and just keep walking around the track."

I'd walk around the track and walk around the track until, finally, I got a little better. Then, Daddy said, "Okay, jog the curves and walk the straightaways." As I got a little bit better, he said, "Okay, jog the straightaways and walk the curves." And, finally, I got good enough that I could jog all the way around, and I was glad for that because I got better. I missed the basketball season, but I was able to play baseball in the spring.

The summer before my senior year, which would be my only season of varsity eligibility, Daddy told me that if I was going to play quarterback, I had to come to the gym every day to go through two sets of passing drills. First, I had to throw a football from about fifteen yards against a mat on the wall fifty times, making sure that it bounced to the left every time. That meant I was putting the proper spin on the ball, making it rotate to the right while keeping the nose up. If the nose is up, the ball bounces to the left. If the nose is down, it bounces to the right.

Then, he wanted me to stand at midcourt and try to put fifty passes into the basket. I don't think I made many of those. I was no Stephen Curry, that's for sure. The idea was just to learn about putting enough arch and touch on the ball to get it to drop through the hoop.

That whole summer, I worked out when nobody was there except the coaches, who were getting ready for the season.

There was another senior starting at quarterback in spring training before my senior year. I knew I was the better player and a lot better athlete, and so did Daddy. But he told me, "Hey, you'll only start if everybody on the team knows that you're the best at that position." The first game of the year, he started the other kid while I started at middle linebacker, which was my other position as one of only three two-way players on the team. We fell behind, so at the half, Dad brought me in at

Showing my wheels at Port Neches-Groves High School.

quarterback. We won the game. I started the rest of the year. More common sense.

In 1965, my senior season, we had a fake field goal play. As the quarterback and holder, I would catch the snap, but instead of placing the ball down for the kick, I'd roll out to my right to throw a pass. The wingback on the left side of the formation would run behind the line all the way to the right and then into the flat to make the reception. We counted on catching the defense by surprise, so no one would be covering the wingback and he'd have a whole bunch of green between him and the end zone.

One day my dad said, "You know, instead of rolling out and throwing it to him, why don't you just pitch it to him as he runs in front of you while you're kneeling down?"

All of us looked at each other and said, "Yeah, why don't we?" We scored a touchdown by doing it Dad's way in our next game. We also used it with the Houston Oilers and scored a touchdown to beat the Chicago Bears. He just had a lot of good advice.

While watching a college game on TV with a friend, Daddy just casually said, "They're going to run around the right end for a touchdown."

"You think so?" his friend said, sounding a little skeptical.

Sure enough, on the next play, that was exactly what happened.

"Bum, how did you know that?"

"Well, there weren't enough defenders on that side to stop the run."

• • •

Each summer, at the Texas High School Coaches Association Convention and Coaching School, Dad's room would be packed. He had a chalkboard in there, and coaches would come in day and night to talk football with him.

In 1957, after his third season at Nederland, Daddy was hired by the legendary Paul "Bear" Bryant as an assistant coach at Texas A&M. Bear didn't know my dad, but he knew he had won all of those games at Nederland.

Bear also liked the numbering system and immediately began using it at A&M, giving Daddy full credit. That's when technique assignments started catching on throughout football. The one thing Bear apparently wasn't all that comfortable with was Dad's nickname. He insisted on calling him "Bun" rather than "Bum," because I guess he thought "Bum" had a negative connotation.

A couple of my most lasting memories of Bear are from a trip I went on with my dad to Jacksonville, Florida, at the end of that first season to watch Texas A&M face Tennessee in the Gator Bowl. I was ten years old, and there's a photo of the three of us, taken before the game, with me wearing this little striped hat like the kind Payne Stewart used to wear when he was golfing.

Coach Bryant never forgot that picture, because every single time I saw him after that, he would bring it up. Even when I was coaching in the NFL and he was well into his legendary, twenty-five-year tenure at Alabama, I'd visit Tuscaloosa on scouting trips and he'd talk about that picture. The other Alabama coaches would actually roll their eyes when they saw me and say, "Oh, no, you're here, and now we're going to have to hear that story about you and that little cap that you wore."

I also was in the locker room before that Gator Bowl when he gave one of the greatest speeches I've ever heard.

"Do you know what they say?" Bear growled in that deep voice of his. Then, he turned to John David Crowe, his half-back who had won the Heisman Trophy and was finishing his junior season.

"They say, 'John David Crowe, all you're thinking about is pro football. You're not thinking about Texas A&M football and this ballgame.'"

Next, Bear turned to Charlie Krueger, his all-American defensive lineman who also was finishing his junior season. "They say, 'You're just thinking about winning the Outland Trophy'"—as the best lineman in the country—"you're not thinking about this team.'"

After that, he pointed to his quarterback, Charlie Milstead, and said "they" were saying he was looking beyond his college career, too. He went right down the line with all the star players, saying "they" said this and "they" said that.

Finally, Bear said, "You know who they are? Me!'" And the guys just went crazy. I mean, it was unbelievable. Although the Aggies would lose the game 3–0, I still get chills just thinking about the speech.

Daddy said when Bear came into a room, everyone would gravitate to him because he was one of those people whose personality made him magnetic. He could be grumpy at times, but he had a special way of making you feel good about what you were doing. Every now and then he would invite my dad or one of the other assistant coaches to join him for lunch, and that would be special because you were getting a private audience with Coach Bryant.

Bear and my dad were similar in a lot of ways. I think they had a good feel for people—how to work with people—and not manipulate them. My dad was young and had a lot of great ideas, and when Coach Bryant left for Alabama after the '57 season, he asked Daddy to go to with him. Daddy turned him down because he said he was "such a Texan" that he didn't want to leave the state.

He took a head coaching job at Jacksonville High School, in Texas, instead. Later, he told me it was one of the biggest mistakes he made because he wanted to be a college head coach, which wouldn't happen for five more years when he got hired at Texas Western. Almost all of the other assistants who went with Bear to Alabama got college head coaching jobs sooner than that.

When I was a senior in high school, Coach Bryant sent me a letter offering me a scholarship to Alabama, sight unseen. He didn't know if I was a good player or not, but he offered me an opportunity to play at one of the top programs in the nation because of his relationship with my dad. But Daddy wasn't going to allow me to go anywhere other than the place he was coaching: the University of Houston, which had an up-and-coming program at the time.

If that wasn't thoughtful enough, Bear sent Laurie and me a gift when we got married in 1969—twelve years after the only season my dad had worked for him.

CHAPTER THREE

"IF IT'S THIRD AND A MILE, WE WON'T GIVE IT TO HIM"

"Defense is so much easier to play than offense.
It's a matter of determination and courage and just
wantin' to. Defense is a guy goin' out there and
reactin' to something. Offense, you've gotta plan
something. It takes 11 people to put a runnin' play
together. One guy can make a tackle."

—Bum Phillips
from *He Ain't No Bum*

Daddy and I like what we've drawn up on the chalkboard.

DADDY NEVER FORCED THE ISSUE OF MY BECOMING A COACH. All he wanted was for me to be honest with myself in choosing it as a career. He knew the demands involved—you couldn't be halfhearted coaching football.

"If this is the only thing you want to do, that you really want to do, then that's what you ought to do," he told me. "But if there's something else that you're thinking about doing, if you think you might want to be an architect or whatever, you shouldn't coach."

I knew coaching was all I wanted to do. I told my son, Wesley, the same thing my dad told me before he became an assistant coach in the NFL.

In 1969, when I was an unpaid graduate assistant at the University of Houston, I got an opportunity to get a high school coaching job in Orange, Texas, from Neil Morgan, who had played for my dad. Bill Yeoman, who was the Houston Cougars' head coach, didn't want me to leave his staff. I was the defensive coordinator of the Houston freshman team and I helped some with the varsity team, which had just won the Bluebonnet Bowl at the Astrodome.

We beat Auburn pretty bad when Pat Sullivan, who won the Heisman Trophy that year, was the Tigers' quarterback. Everybody was kind of excited about the University of Houston and what we were doing, so when Bill asked me to stay on, I thought, "Wow! This is pretty good."

Then I called my dad, who was defensive coordinator for the San Diego Chargers at the time, to see what he thought.

"What are you gettin' paid at the University of Houston?" he asked.

"Nothing," I said. "Room and board."

Walking down the aisle with the love of my life, Laurie, on March 29, 1969.

"Well, one of 'em's paying and one of 'em isn't. You'd better take the one that's paying."

Even with the salary jump from zero to $12,000, you would naturally think that being in college is better than high school, especially when it came to getting noticed by other colleges. But my dad put those concerns to rest. "They'll find you," he told me. "If you're a good coach, they'll find you."

I took the high school job. Neil Morgan had a brilliant football mind. I think that was part of my dad's thinking, too. He trusted that Neil could teach me a lot of football and a lot of things about coaching.

The money wasn't bad, either. Laurie and I had just gotten married, and she was making about $8,000 or $9,000 teaching. We lived in an apartment, had no kids, and paid for everything with cash. I always joke that we had more then than we have now.

As someone who was just starting out, my main responsibility at Orange High School that first season was scouting the upcoming opponent. That meant every Friday night I would be at a different game than ours. One week, the team I was supposed to scout had an open date, so Neil had me sit in the press box for our game. I wore a headset and sent some plays down to the field that ended up working.

We won the game. Afterward, Neil said, "You're not going on the road anymore." He put me in the press box for the rest of the season.

I had a feel for the game, and with all of the opponents I scouted, I knew the plays they were running. I could anticipate what they were going to do based on formations and so forth. I was literally able to tell the coaches down the field, "Hey, they're going to run this play next time." Sure enough, they did. Joe Washington was at Lincoln High School in Port Arthur that year. We held him without a touchdown, which was pretty amazing against a running back who would go on to have a great career at Oklahoma and in the NFL.

There were two high schools in Orange—Orange and West Orange. Orange was integrated and the district was poorer. West Orange wasn't integrated, but after that first season, the school board wanted to integrate West Orange. We had many more African American players at Orange, and the powers behind West Orange gerrymandered the district lines.

That allowed West Orange to take almost every player that we had. I'm talking about first-team players. Neil Morgan went into a big tirade and ended up quitting over it. Dexter Bassinger, the offensive coordinator, took over as head coach, and named me defensive coordinator.

My dad came back from San Diego to watch one of our games and saw me coaching. I heard from other coaches later on that he said, "Hey, Wade's going to be a really good coach."

Back then, it wasn't his way to give me a direct compliment, which I think had more to do with his generation than anything else. When he got older, he told me he was proud of me. If anybody asked him about me later on, he would say, "Well, he knows everything I know and he knows everything he knows, so that's why he's a great coach."

I had finished my second season as defensive coordinator at Orange High School when Dad, having become the defensive coordinator at Oklahoma State, gave me a call that went something like this.

"You're coaching linebackers at Oklahoma State," he said. "Get up here!"

"Okay."

That was a great experience. I was twenty-four years old and coaching in the Big Eight Conference. That's when I really learned the most football. There was another young coach on the staff, Harold Richardson, who had come along with my dad from SMU. Harold and I would always argue about football stuff, and then my dad would jump in and say, "Hey, you know, this is the way you do this, this is the way you do that."

I got to talk more football with Dad as a grown football coach. There were more conversations about technique and I was able to learn about the things he knew. All of us who were younger guys on the staff would get advice from him. It was more along the lines of how to do things, what techniques to use, how to teach players to do things better, what makes them more efficient, how to get them to be better players.

Dad had a different theory than most coaches. He wasn't as cookie cutter as everybody else. He thought, Well, if a guy can do this, then you ought to let him do it. If a guy can't do that, you need to teach him to do something different or better.

After only one season, Daddy left Oklahoma State. His replacement was Lance VanZandt. He was from Port Neches, so my dad and I had known him for a long time. I was looking forward to working with him. Lance was brilliant. You wouldn't know it if you talked to him, but he had tremendous intellect. He was what I would call "goofy smart."

He had all of these sayings. If something came up, like the number nine for a nine-on-nine drill, he'd say, "Nine-on-nine that pal of mine, bluebird shit on a frozen line." It didn't mean anything, but he'd say stuff like that every time. After he got out of coaching, he started playing bridge and was a top amateur player.

We had a good season that ended with us playing in the Fiesta Bowl, where we beat seventeenth-ranked BYU as an unranked team. After that, the University of Kansas hired Lance to become defensive coordinator, and offered him a nice pay raise. He took the job and brought me along to be his defensive line coach. I got a pay raise, too.

When my dad was with the Chargers, he sent me a film reel he'd spliced together of all of the top defensive linemen in the National Football League of that era—guys like Deacon Jones and Bob Lilly—rushing the passer. I studied that reel over and over and over and over, and I felt like I learned how those guys were rushing the passer and what it took to be able to rush the passer. Although they were great players, there were certain fundamentals in their game that I felt I could teach to another player even if he didn't have as much ability.

For instance, Deacon Jones had his signature head slap. The NFL would eventually outlaw it, but at the time it was viewed as a great tactic. He would take one of those big hands of his, bring it up from way down low and slap the offensive lineman in the side of the helmet. That would cause the other player to have ringing in his ears and become disoriented. Then Deacon turned his hips and his body, to where they were more angled toward the quarterback. Instead of running straight up the field like everyone else, he was taking angles.

Everybody thinks pass rushing is all about having moves, like the swim and the club and all that stuff. But you've also got to get the correct angles. Bob Lilly could turn his shoulders so much that it changed the angle of where the offensive lineman was, and where he could go. I started teaching defensive linemen to turn their hips and use their shoulders. I gained a lot of confidence in my ability to coach the pass rush.

I also had a lot of confidence in my attire. I just believed I could look good in anything I wore. One day, I received a multicolored leisure suit from my dad. Little did I know that he had gotten it for himself, but being color-blind, he had no idea how loud those colors really were. Not until he wore it in front of the players and they started laughing like crazy. Dad had the kind of relationship with players where they felt they could tease him and it would all be in good fun.

One day, while I was at Kansas and made a recruiting trip to Houston, I wore the leisure suit because I thought it looked really good on me. I stopped by an Oilers practice, and the players started falling down laughing. I had no idea why.

Then one of them said, "Bum, you did it! You pawned that thing off on Wade." Hey, I still thought I looked good in it.

The highlight of that 1975 season at Kansas was our 23–3 upset win at Oklahoma. It was considered one of the biggest upsets in college football at the time. The Sooners had won twenty-eight straight games and were the second-ranked team in the country. They finished 11–1 and were national champions, but they also were voted the most disappointing team in the Big 8 because of that loss to us.

We wound up 7–5 and played in the Sun Bowl in El Paso, Texas, where I saw the exact opposite of Daddy's coaching philosophy. Our opponent was Pittsburgh, which had future Pro Football Hall-of-Famer Tony Dorsett at running back. Bud Moore, our head coach, believed that you needed to be a hard ass to be successful. We took our blocking sleds to El Paso, because Bud was going to make sure that in the weeks leading up to the game, we were going full bore with our hitting.

Pitt's players were going out around town, enjoying themselves, while our guys weren't having any fun at all. Part of the whole bowl game experience is to have fun in the days leading up to the game. Bud tried to tell us we were doing it the right way, but Pitt beat us with a really good team.

• • •

Bud was tough on our players, because that was the way he believed he should coach. He was a great guy to work for, but I never felt the players got to see that side of him.

After only one year at OSU, Daddy returned to the NFL in 1974 when Sid Gillman took over as head coach of the Oilers. He again made Dad his defensive coordinator. One of the funniest stories I ever heard from that season was when Sid told my dad that breaking down game tape was better than sex.

"Well, Sid," Dad said, "either I don't know how to watch film or you don't know how to make love."

Only a year after arriving in Houston, Sid stepped down as head coach but stayed on as GM. Bud Adams, the Oilers' owner, offered Dad the job to replace Sid as head coach. Now, here was my dad, being offered his first head coaching job of an

That's bubble gum, NOT tobacco, in that jaw!

NFL team, so you would think he'd be jumping at the opportunity, right? He wasn't.

"Bud, I'm not going to sign this contract unless it says I have control over the players, who we have on the team, and all that," my dad said.

Bud went along with it. A short while later, Sid came up to Daddy and said, "Well, we're going to do this with this player, this player, and this player."

"Sid, have you looked at my contract?"

"No."

"Well, you need to look at it."

Sid looked at the contract and quit that day. Daddy hadn't even been head coach of the Oilers for one game yet, and now he was their head coach and general manager.

When I was twenty-seven years old, Daddy called me up and said, "You're coming to the Oilers." There wasn't much else I was going to say except, "Okay."

He had confidence in me, and believed that I could handle the job. I had confidence in him, and believed that he wouldn't have given me a job if he didn't think I could handle it. I also had confidence in myself, and believed that I could handle it.

At first, my dad had to hire me as linebackers coach. I say "had to," because the guy who was coaching the defensive line had been a backup player in 1975. Bud Adams, the team owner, still owed him another year's salary, so he wanted Bum to keep him as defensive line coach for that one season. The guy had never coached before and it showed. I had only been coaching in high school and college, but I knew right away he wasn't a good coach. The players just ran all over him.

Those guys on the defensive line had pretty strong personalities. You had Curley Culp, who was one of the best nose tackles in the game. Bubba Smith was there, too, nearing the end of a nine-year career. So was his brother, Tody, who was really wild. That first year I was there Curley wouldn't talk to me. My personality being what it is, every time I saw him, I'd say, "Hey, Curley! How you doin', man?" He would just sort of growl.

After that year, my dad brought me into his office and said, "Wade, you're going to coach the defensive line this year."

"Well, that's good," I said. "Because Curley and I really get along well."

Daddy knew I was joking, of course, because Curley wasn't getting along well with anybody. He seemed like he was mad at the world. But Curley was really smart. When I started coaching the defensive line, I'd tell him, "Hey, we've got to do this, or play this technique this way." And he'd say, "Well, I'm getting double-teamed." And I'd say, "Well, Curley, if you get double-teamed on this, that means somebody on our defense is free to make the play."

Teams did double-team him a lot, and he always griped about it. But he knew that if we did certain things, I would explain them to him and he would understand why we were doing them. That's what my dad always said. You don't just coach a guy and tell him the stuff. You try to explain it to him, give him the why and how and its purpose in the defense overall. The smart ones obviously realize that.

The player who balked the most at my coaching that first year was Tody Smith. In those days, you didn't have as many players on your roster, so in order to do drills, you needed some players at your position to be "show" guys—playing the part of the opponents to show what they would do to counter what you were doing on a particular side of the ball. In our case, we needed three defensive linemen to be offensive linemen. All they had to do was go through the motions of blocking. It

wasn't anything too taxing. But one day, after I told Tody to be one of the "show" guys, he said, "I'm not doing that."

I said, "You need to do this, because when it's your turn, you're going to be on defense, and we're going to have someone else from this group show you. We just don't have enough people to do it another way." He still wouldn't do it. I knew he was testing me, seeing how far he could push it. I didn't back down. I told him to go stand on the sideline by himself and we finished the drill.

The next day, Tody did everything. I found out the other guys had gone up to him and said, "Hey, that isn't the right way. You need to do what the rest of us do." I think that was a defining moment for me as a coach at that time.

The Oilers players hadn't really been coached. You didn't see a lot of detailed coaching overall in pro football at that time. What most NFL coaches did back then was just teach assignment football. They were just telling players, "Hey, you got this guy, man to man." There weren't any fundamentals involved, like staying low or showing them how to pass rush. Nobody was telling them, "Well, you've got to keep your feet under you, with your weight on your inside step." Or, "Mirror this." Or, "This should be your hand placement on this stuff." Or, "You've got this gap, you've got that gap."

Even something as basic as how to tackle wasn't being taught. The players would just be told, "Go tackle the guy." They didn't have any drills on how to tackle. They didn't even use a tackling dummy or anything. I just didn't think they were coached at all, because the NFL coaches assumed they already knew the fundamentals and didn't bother to work with them to sharpen their skills.

Coming from high school and college, I was already of the belief that you had to do a lot of teaching with football players, because in high school and college, you've got to make them better. With pro football, coaches always said, "OK, if you can't do it, we'll get somebody else." Some pro coaches at the time, especially ones that had played in the NFL, would also tell players, "Hey, you go cover that guy." They wouldn't tell them how to do it. They wouldn't show them in drills how to make them do it better. They would just say, "Go do it!"

That all would change when the salary cap came in, because then you started losing players. When you bring somebody in, first of all, it can cost more money and not be a good fit under your salary cap. Secondly, you've still got to coach them enough to get them as good as the guy they replaced. Like Daddy always said, "You've got to get the average player to play good and the good player to play great."

A player who needed a lot of coaching was future Hall of Fame defensive end Elvin Bethea, who had been an offensive guard in college. I was teaching fundamentals of stunting, which is when a defensive end lines up outside of an offensive tackle and then on the snap of the ball, moves to the inside. I'd say, "Alright, on this stunt, I want you to step at a forty-five-degree angle, slide down the line, keep your shoulders square, and then go through the hole."

During one practice, he stepped at the wrong angle coming off the line and I showed him how to do it the right way and then told him to do it again. He did it wrong again. Once more, I pointed out what the mistake was and how to correct it.

Finally, on the third try, he got it right and I said, "That's great!" Elvin looked up at the big tower from where my dad coached practice and hollered, "Hey, Bum! Wade's here coaching his ass off!"

Dad just laughed, and so did everybody else at practice.

My dad and I liked the 3–4 defense, because it's good against the run, which most college offenses featured back in the day. It's a more mobile defense. In the 4–3, you've got four linemen who don't move as well as four linebackers. It's an even better defense in pro football, because the NFL is such a passing league. The 3–4 lets you do a better job of getting pressure than the 4–3.

In the 4–3, you know where the four guys are coming from. In a 3–4, you know three of them are coming, but you don't know where the other one is coming from. It might be one of the two inside 'backers, it might be the weak-side 'backer, or it might be the strong-side 'backer. At the time, that was foreign to all of the older coaches, so it really compromised their ability to put blockers in the right position to protect the quarterback.

The first year the Oilers used the 3–4, Ted Washington, who played outside linebacker, got like ten sacks. Back then, sacks weren't recognized as an official statistic, but believe me,

Ted got at least that many. On most of them, he was blocked, because opponents knew they had to do something to try to keep him off of the quarterback. But it usually didn't matter, because he weighed 250–255 pounds and was strong as hell.

• • •

My dad would always say I was a heck of a judge of talent. He believed he was good at it, too. This is what Daddy had to say about evaluating players after the NFL decided in 1977 to reduce the preseason schedule from six games to four and increase the regular-season schedule from fourteen games to sixteen: "Aw, heck, if you can't figure out in two weeks of practice and four preseason games whether some rookie's got what you're lookin' for, you ain't a coach and ain't never gonna be. And if you can't show your stuff in that time, you ain't the kind of player any coach is gonna want."*

The kind of players Dad wanted were ones that would always give you a full game, no matter the circumstances. Too hot. Too cold. Too sore.

"Ask our scouts," he said. "When we go 'round and look at college players, we don't ask if they can play with a little pain. We ask 'em, 'Do they practice with it?' If they practice with it, I know damn well they'll play with it."*

As coaches, we had to go out on the road to different schools to look at players for the draft. You looked at every player on the team, not just the ones at your position or on your side of the ball. You also looked at all of the players on the teams the school played against. One of my schools was Tulsa. Once we were into the draft and we got to the fourth round, I said, "I think this receiver they got at Tulsa is really a good player, and we ought to draft him." We ended up drafting Steve Largent.

At the end of training camp, we were in a meeting and Bum said, "Well, we need to cut a receiver. Who are we going to cut?" One of the coaches said, "Largent, Steve Largent, because we have Otis Taylor, who is going to come back from an injury." That's when I realized, *You ought to say something.*

Before I could speak, another assistant coach, Richie Petitbon, who was sitting next to me, stood up and he said, "Coach, that kid catches every ball from behind his back...We can't cover him."

Then I said, "He might not be that fast, but I'm telling you, we can't cover him in a practice."

My dad asked the receiver coach and the offensive coordinator, "Well, what about that? You think we ought to keep him or not?"

"No, no," they said. "He's not good enough."

We waived Steve, Seattle claimed him, and then we recalled him from waivers and worked out a trade with the Seahawks. We ended up getting a third-round draft pick. We thought we did alright. We didn't do alright. After Largent finished playing for the Seahawks, he got a bronze bust in the Pro Football Hall of Fame.

In 1978, before my third season with the Oilers, all of the scouts and coaches were in the draft room to discuss our plans for the draft. We were picking seventeenth overall, so we all assumed we wouldn't be talking about the guys we had rated in the top ten. We certainly thought it would be a big waste of time to talk about Earl Campbell, the Heisman Trophy-winning running back from Texas that every team projected as the top overall pick.

Then, all of a sudden, my dad said, "Why don't we talk about this guy right here." He pointed to Earl Campbell's nameplate, sitting right at the top of our draft board. The room got quiet.

"How many of you have seen Earl Campbell in person?" Daddy said. Six or seven of the scouts and coaches, excluding me, raised their hands.

My dad said, "I've got one question for you guys: Do you think he's the best player that you've ever seen?"

I'm thinking, *Wait a minute. The best player I've ever seen?* The names started running through my mind...Jim Brown... Johnny Unitas. Is my dad seriously putting Earl Campbell, a guy who had yet to play a single down in the NFL, in that category already?

King Hill, who was our offensive coordinator and a former NFL quarterback, was sitting next to me. He was one of the guys who raised his hand.

"Coach, I can't say he isn't," King said.

"What?" I said.

King turned toward me and said, "Wade, he's uncanny."

"Awww, come on now."

I had seen Earl on TV and I knew he'd won the Heisman and all that stuff. I also knew that we had a scout who gave him a grade of 9.8 or 9.9 out of 10, which was unheard of. But I had to see for myself what the others saw and why they were so over the top about him.

One of the schools I was responsible for scouting was Notre Dame, which had beaten Texas in the Cotton Bowl that year. Earl had 116 yards rushing in that game. I had been focusing on Notre Dame's defense, which was really good that year. I watched every game from Notre Dame's season on film, because there were about eight guys from that defense who were going to be drafted.

After hearing what King Hill said and thinking about that

scout's near-perfect grade, I made a special trip to Notre Dame to rewatch the film of the Cotton Bowl, this time concentrating on Earl. What I saw was that the guy was just running over and through people. Nobody on that defense was blocked. I mean, Texas's offensive line didn't block a damn soul, and he was still making five or six yards on almost every carry. I had thought Notre Dame did a good job of stopping him. I thought Notre Dame beat Earl Campbell.

They didn't really beat him. It was like he was super human. It was unbelievable.

I was thinking about what King had said in that meeting. After giving it a little more thought, I said to myself, *Nope, I've never seen anyone this good. Maybe he is the best that ever played.* Earl had almost a hundred yards on the ground at the half, but Texas was behind so they didn't run the ball much the rest of the game.

I went back to my hotel room and I called Laurie.

"Hey, babe," I said.

Before I could get another word out, she said, "Isn't it great?"

"What? Isn't what great?"

"We got Earl Campbell."

"What are you talking about?"

"You haven't heard?"

"No."

"We traded with Tampa for the number one pick."

For a moment, I was speechless. Then I let out a "WOOOOOO!" and started jumping up and down. I think the other hotel guests thought I was having a heart attack or something, but I couldn't believe this had happened—to me, to us, to the whole deal. We gave the Buccaneers a tight end, Jimmie Giles, our first- and second-round picks in the 1978 draft, and our third- and fifth-round picks in 1979. Daddy called it a "commitment to excellence." I just thought it was fantastic. Earl was the greatest player I had ever seen. And now he was on our team.

In building his roster, Daddy's first priority was to try to get good players through the draft and with trades. But I think he was more responsible for the good chemistry that we had rather than the actual makeup of the players he selected. It came from the way he treated people, the way we practiced, the way we had fun doing things. For instance, he would have ice cream one day at practice, just to give the guys a little treat for working hard. My dad helped them enjoy playing football.

The players always knew he was on their side. At the start of training camp one summer, Earl failed to complete the mile run to test the players' physical condition. Reporters covering the team went crazy. They were all chasing after my dad, saying, "Bum! Bum! Earl didn't finish the mile run. What are you going to do?"

Dad gave one of his classic common-sense answers.

"Hell, if it's third and a mile, we won't give it to him," he told them. "But we're going to give it to him the rest of the time."

We had a bunch of characters on that team, and Daddy had no problem letting them be themselves. Dan Pastorini, our Hall of Fame quarterback, really liked going out on the town and having a good time. Dad's only concern was that he showed up where he needed to be when he needed to be there, and was ready to play on Sunday. He talked to all of the players a lot about not only discipline, but self-discipline. He told them what was important—which was to practice and play hard—and if whatever they were doing on their own time didn't take away from anything football-wise, he didn't care. I think the players respected him enough to listen.

Toni Fritsch, our kicker, was a different kind of guy, which

Bum believed that you could always find a little time to relax.

might not be saying a whole lot because kickers are all pretty different people anyway. But Toni was strange in the sense that he kicked the ball just hard enough to get it over the crossbar. No matter the distance, it would just barely go over. You'd see that on extra points. You'd move it back to thirty yards, move it back to fifty yards, and it would barely go over. Sometimes, in practice, Toni would kick forty or fifty field goals in a row and when that got monotonous for him, he'd practice hitting the crossbar for a while.

Toni and Pastorini used to bet each other on who could hit the crossbar more times from like twenty-five yards away, with Toni kicking and Dan throwing. Sometimes Fritch won, I mean, it was amazing. He kicked it just hard enough, but he knew exactly where it was going to go.

We had Billy "White Shoes" Johnson, one of the all-time best kick returners in the game, known for those low-cut white shoes he wore and for being one of the first players to do an end-zone celebration dance. On his returns, he did all kinds of zigging and zagging, turning and spinning, changing directions a bunch of times. When he got to the end zone, he would put on another show by doing a dance called the Funky Chicken. He'd get up on his toes and bend both legs in and out with his hands raised, one holding the ball. Then he'd do a couple of splits before acting like he was going to throw the ball, but he'd actually let it fall behind his back while moving his arm forward. It was a lot of fun to watch, unless you were the other team.

"When Billy gets his hands on the ball, the main thing is to get out of his way because there's no tellin' when he's gonna come back in your direction," Daddy said. "When Billy gets his hands on the ball, it's look out time. We don't even know where he's gonna go…As for that little dance he does in the end zone, he's a favorite of so many people that he can do damn near what he wants to do. They might not like it if somebody else did it, but he can do it. He can do anything."*

Daddy liked to say there are two kinds of football players that "ain't worth a damn: one that never does what he's told and the other that never does anything except what he's told." I always believed that to be true. If you've got a great pass rusher, like a Bruce Smith, a lot of old-school coaches would say, "You've got to contain rush," meaning that as you rush the passer, you also have to make sure you're containing the out-side to make sure the quarterback stays in the pocket. If you go inside, you run the risk possibly getting caught out of position if the quarterback scrambles.

But with a Bruce Smith or a Reggie White or a Ricky Jackson, you let them go get the quarterback any way they could. You give them the leeway to do it any way they like, because they're that good.

Now, to somebody that's not a great pass rusher, you say, "Hey, you contain rush, don't let them out of the pocket." With some coaches, that's all they'll say, no matter who the players are. But when you've got a Bruce Smith, you say, "You rush. Even though we're worried about getting containment, I think you're going to make the right decision, when you go inside, that you're going to get the quarterback."

They have to have some kind of football initiative, as long as it's something you know they can do. If they can't, they can't, and you've got to tell them to do it a different way. You don't want that guy who does everything you say because he isn't even going to try to make plays unconventionally to show you—and himself—that he can. The guy who does nothing you say is just not disciplined.

When Bruce Smith had a chance to beat the offensive tackle inside and make the play, he did. Some guys can cover a guy really well and break on the ball really well and they play the receiver differently than other guys that don't have the same skills. You tell him, "Hey, you play it the way you play it, that's what you're good at."

You've got to recognize what a player does best and what he can do that other players can't, and you allow him to use those things. It's not just the Xs and the Os; it's the Moes and Joes. You can play the same technique, the same assignment, but you can also allow certain players to do it a different way because players aren't all the same. If I had a good player, I'd let him be a good player.

If I had someone at cornerback like Quentin Jammer, who I coached in San Diego, I'd let him do exactly what his name and his skill set said he could do: jam people at the line of scrimmage. When we played zone, he jammed them at the line of scrimmage. When we played man, he jammed them at the line of scrimmage. Because that's what he did really well. Now, when he played off the line, which is how most corners are going to play in zone coverage, he didn't do as well.

When I was with the Texans, we let J.J. Watt, one of the most talented defensive linemen I've ever seen, do a lot of things. When the ball is going away from him and a guy's trying to block him, he'll run around behind the block and make the play. To almost every coach, that's a cardinal sin, because the back will hit the seam that J.J. creates by going outside for a long gain. But J.J. can run around and still make the play before the back hits the seam.

If you're just an old-time or hardline coach, you say, "No, we don't want you doing that! Don't do that anymore!" What we say is, "If you can do that again, do it again." Which he can.

Elvin Bethea and Curley Culp were that type of player for us with the Oilers. Greg Kragen, who I had in my first stint with the Broncos, made the Pro Bowl as a noseguard even though he was undersized. We let him stunt all the time because he was tremendous at stunting. We always put Ted Washington, who we had in Buffalo, right over the center, because he was so big and strong and capable of overpowering most centers or dealing with double-team blocks when one of the guards helped out.

These players play in the same positions as other players. They play the same responsibilities. They just play them different ways because they're different players. You have to let them play.

It doesn't mean you're just letting the players do their own thing. It means you're getting the best out of them because they have a chance to do the things they do well. That's a philosophy I learned from Daddy.

As he said: "You have to be organized, but we're not a slave to organization. You don't want to be so damn organized that a guy feels like a puppet on a string. You gotta have guys that got enough…uh, nerve or somethin' to take a chance. I don't mean gamblers. I mean guys that will take a risk as long as it's a calculated risk."*

CHAPTER FOUR

LOVE YA BLUE

"Everybody says, 'Ya'll gotta play Pittsburgh twice.' I like to think, 'Pittsburgh's gotta play us twice, too.'"

—Bum Phillips
from *He Ain't No Bum*

How about that belt buckle?

By the 1978 season, the Oilers' popularity had climbed to heights never before seen in Houston. There was a slogan, "Love Ya Blue," that our public relations guy, Jack Cherry, coined and it caught on in a big way. Fans showed up at our games carrying cards with "Love Ya Blue" in big letters. They waved blue and white pom-poms. They had their faces painted with the Oilers' logo on their cheeks. They sang fight songs. It felt a lot more like a college than a professional atmosphere.

Houston's economy was doing really well because the energy business was thriving, so a lot of people were moving there from all over because there were so many jobs available. With all of this growth taking place, the Oilers gave the community something to rally around. And Daddy was at the center of it all. Fans not only loved the fact that we were winning, they also loved that Daddy was a real cowboy at a time when you were

Just a couple of urban cowboys.

starting to see a whole bunch of "urban" cowboys everywhere. A couple of years later, there would be a movie based on that whole culture, *Urban Cowboy*, with John Travolta.

Everybody had gone cowboy crazy before then. Our whole football team wore cowboy hats when we were on the road. We were all wearing cowboy boots. The difference with Daddy was that he had been wearing cowboy boots and a ten-gallon hat for most of his life. He always wore his hat on the sidelines if we weren't playing at home in the Astrodome…because his momma wouldn't let him wear a hat indoors.

A big part of the excitement among the fans came from our rivalry with the Pittsburgh Steelers. It wasn't just because we were in the AFC Central together and always had those two regular-season games against each other. It was also because we saw them as the team to beat, like every team in the NFL. That was in the era when the Steelers won all four of the Super Bowls they appeared in during a six-year span. They were the team you had to beat to get to the Super Bowl.

It was a friendly rivalry rather than a we-hate-you, you-hate-us kind of deal. In 1977, we beat another division opponent in the last game of the year, the Cincinnati Bengals. That gave the Steelers the division title and put them in the playoffs. Had the Bengals won, the Steelers would have missed the postseason. At the time, the Steelers were featured in a television commercial for Samsonite luggage. That was the one with the players in their uniforms, pads, and helmets, diving on, jumping on, kicking, and throwing suitcases all over a football field. As a thank you for beating the Bengals, they sent Samsonite briefcases to all of our players and coaches.

Daddy and Terry Bradshaw, the Steelers' great quarterback, were friends. In fact, Daddy gave him a pair of cowboy boots before one of our games.

"Bum Phillips is a guy I'm just naturally drawn to because of his personality, his warmth, his friendliness, his honesty," Terry said. "I mean he's so doggone sincere. I love him. It's like a father-son relationship, even though I play for probably the Oilers' biggest rival. He's the kind of guy you'd go to war for, fight for, give your life for. I have the utmost respect for him. I'm crazy about the guy. He's a super human being. It's nice to know there are coaches in our business who love their players. He can get more out of them without hollering than anybody I've ever seen. It would be very easy to get up and play for him."*

After he got out of football, Daddy did several speaking engagements in Pittsburgh. The people up there liked him. After a game in Pittsburgh, a fan ran onto the field and stole his cowboy hat as he was coming off the field. About a week or so later, he got it back in the mail. There was a note with it that said, "Sorry about that. Pittsburgh Steelers fans."

My father's respect for the Steelers started when he first went to work for the Oilers in 1974. He never forgot a conversation he had with Joe Greene, one of the mainstays of the

Steel Curtain defense, after the Oilers won in Pittsburgh late that season.

"They needed that ballgame," Daddy recalled. "They hadn't won the Super Bowl yet and they were strugglin' to get into the playoffs. We beat 'em in a ballgame that had to mean a whole lot to them, a lot more to them than it did to us because we were out of it."

"Well, Joe Greene came up to me after the game and said, 'Coach, be sure to congratulate ol' number seven [Dan Pastorini] because he's been through a whole lot and he's never gotten down. He's always gotten up off the ground and he hasn't had a lot of protection. He's a real competitor. I'm proud of him.' Here he was, genuinely hurtin' because they just got beat, but, at the same time, he could be proud for somebody else. The Terry Bradshaws, the Joe Greenes, a lot of 'em in this league… hell, they're the same kind of people we got. They're the same players we got 'cept they got a different color hat on."*

Facing all of those Hall of Famers was a tremendous challenge—Bradshaw, Greene, Franco Harris, Lynn Swann, John Stallworth, Mike Webster, Mel Blount, Jack Lambert, Jack Ham. But we were a pretty good team, too. We split with them every year I was there, 1976 to 1980.

Our main focus defensively against the Steelers was the same as it was against everybody else: we had to stop them from running the ball, and we did a pretty good job of that. For one thing, we were a top-ten defense. For another, we had a strong front and we were playing a 3–4, which at the time was different than what the Steelers saw from most of their opponents.

The Steelers trapped everybody in their run game. They were tremendous at that. They were the best trapping team that I've ever seen. If you play against the trap as a defensive line, you've got to stay on the line of scrimmage. If you go upfield to rush the passer, you get trapped and you're taken out of the play. They trapped everybody they could—the noseguards, the ends. And then Franco Harris or Rocky Bleier—but mostly Franco— was running for a big gain.

I haven't seen anything like it since. I've seen great running teams that helped their passing game because they made you commit too much to stopping the run, but this was different. You want to get to the quarterback, but then you know they're looking to knock you out of the play and then they're going to run inside of you. We also didn't play against teams that trapped all the time, so it was different for us.

Trapping against a 3–4 defense was a little different and probably harder for them because they mostly played 4–3 teams. They tried to trap Curley Culp, or run what's called a "wham" on him. That's where no one blocks the noseguard, and then the tight end comes off the line and hits the noseguard running up the middle. They only tried that a few times with Curley. I think the tight end said, "Hey, let's don't do that anymore," because Curley knocked him backwards every time into the ball carrier.

It was hard for our offense to move the ball against that Steel Curtain defense, so our defense was on the field more against Pittsburgh than it was against other teams. In Earl Campbell's first game against the Steelers as a rookie, we beat them in Pittsburgh and he had eighty-nine yards. He didn't have any-thing close to that in most of his other games against them, and you're talking about a guy who led the league in rushing in each of his first three NFL seasons. They were that good on defense.

The Steelers wound up losing to the Broncos in the '77 playoffs, but the next couple years we played them in the AFC Championship Game. Both times we played in Pittsburgh and both times we lost, 34–5 and 27–13. Before the 1978 AFC title game, Daddy told reporters, "Playin' Pittsburgh is like eatin' an ice cream cone on a hot summer day. Sometime before you can get it all in your mouth, it gets all over ya."

After each of those conference-championship losses, fans in Houston greeted us to show their appreciation for the seasons we'd had. One of the most unforgettable moments of my life was after that first loss to the Steelers in the AFC title game. On the flight back from Pittsburgh, my dad said, "Well, we promised that we were gonna meet the fans at the Astrodome, win or lose, so we're going to go." Our normal routine after coming back from road games was to get on buses at the airport and go to the facility, where our cars were parked. No one was interested in making the detour to the Astrodome. Besides, our plane was three hours late leaving Pittsburgh.

"We don't want to go, Coach," players and coaches, including me, were telling him. "Nobody's going to be there, anyway, because we lost."

"No," he said. "We gave our word that we're gonna go, so we're gonna go."

Tracy, Wes, and I can't wait to get into that birthday cake... especially me.

We landed, got on the buses, and as we got close to the Astrodome, we noticed there were cars all over the parking lot. There wasn't anyone directing people where to park, so they just left their cars everywhere, in all directions. Our buses were having a hard time weaving through them, and that was when we started to realize that there might be more people showing up than any of us expected. There was a ramp leading through a tunnel to the field, and it opened up for our buses.

As each one drove onto the field, that was when bedlam broke out. It was unbelievable. The stadium was packed with fifty thousand people. They had been waiting three hours for us. They were waving pom-poms and cheering like crazy. It was amazing and very emotional. You looked around and players had tears in their eyes. We all did.

• • •

After the 1979 season, we pulled off one of the biggest playoff upsets ever when we beat the Chargers at San Diego, 17–14. That was when three key members of our starting offense—Earl Campbell, Dan Pastorini and wide receiver Kenny Burrough— didn't play because of injuries. The Chargers had a Hall of Fame quarterback, Dan Fouts, who had set an NFL record during the season by throwing for 4,082 yards. They had the Air Coryell offense, because their coach, Don Coryell, liked to throw the ball a ton, and he had the quarterback and receivers to do it. I'm sure we were twenty-point underdogs at least. That win was nothing short of a miracle.

Our strong safety, Vernon Perry, had four interceptions and blocked a field goal that he ran back fifty-seven yards to set up a field goal for us. Vernon wasn't an All-Pro or a Pro Bowler, but in my mind he had the greatest game of any defensive player in the history of football. And we won with a backup quarterback, Gifford Nielsen.

Daddy never talked to any of his teams about winning and losing. He would always tell his players, "Hey, you play as hard as you can play, you play as good as you can play, you get ready to play and the scoreboard will take care of itself." He never did say, "We're gonna win the game if you do all that."

Now, the night before the San Diego game, as we were talking in his hotel room, he said, "We're gonna beat 'em."

"Well, yeah, of course," I said. "And they're probably thinking the same thing."

"No, we're gonna beat them. You know why?"

"No, I don't. I mean, hopefully, we play good."

"No, that's not what I'm talking about. Take a look at this."

He handed me the sports page from a San Diego newspaper.

"There's not one word in there about us," Daddy said. "It's about them being the number one seed, them already having beaten the best teams they could play, it's all about them. Nothing was said about us. That's the way you get your ass beat."

"Well, okay."

The next day, we went out and played like crazy. Without Earl Campbell, without Dan Pastorini, without Kenny Burrough.

The Steelers would end up beating the Los Angeles Rams in the Super Bowl. During the regular season, the Chargers had beaten the Steelers by twenty-eight points and the Rams by twenty-four. So when you think about it, we were really the second-best team in the league that year.

The fans came up big again after our second straight AFC title loss to the Steelers. That was when Bum gave what will always be remembered as "the Speech." He told the crowd, "Last year we knocked on the door. This year, we beat on the door. Next year, we're gonna kick the son of a bitch in!"

The next year, we actually beat the Steelers 6–0 in Houston to knock them out of the playoffs. We finished 11–5 and tied with the Cleveland Browns for best record in the AFC Central, but lost the division championship on a tiebreaker. We then lost a wild card playoff game at Oakland, 27–7.

Afterward, there was an uproar. "Oh, my gosh! You lost a wild card game now, instead of the championship game!" There were negative things written in the Houston papers, but we all figured that things would calm down.

Well, they didn't. Three days later, on New Year's Eve, all of us on the coaching staff started getting phone calls from reporters saying, "Hey, Bum's being fired." Supposedly Bud Adams, the team owner, had told some people at a party that he was going to fire Dad and word spread from there. What was terrible was Dad heard about it on the radio before going into the office the next day and hearing directly from Bud.

As soon as they fired Bum, the outrage over us losing to the Raiders just went the opposite way. People went, "Wait a minute here, that's crazy." Everybody was shocked that even after all of the winning we had done, my dad was losing his job. Oakland went on to win the Super Bowl that year, so that meant we lost to the Super Bowl champion three years in a row in the playoffs.

We were probably the second-best team in football, but that didn't stop Bud from firing my dad. The reason he pointed to was that we couldn't win the AFC title game, we couldn't get over that hump, and losing in the wild card round meant we were going in the wrong direction.

I think there was a little more to it than that. My own personal feeling was that Bud maybe got a little tired of all of the attention Bum was getting. It was a "Luv Ya Blue," Bum

Phillips's Oilers kind of deal. It had always been Bud Adams's Oilers in the past, but fans recognized Bum as the face of the organization. They felt a real connection with him, like he was one of them. Ladd Herzeg was another factor. He was a behind-the-scenes, cutthroat guy who was the general manager on the business side and wanted more power. He was the pencil pusher while Daddy was the GM making all of the important football decisions. Ladd didn't like that.

Bum took the firing in stride. He said, "Hey, Bud's the owner, he can do anything he wants to. He owns the team; I worked as hard as I could every day. He paid me, and he paid me for every day I worked. That was it."

He had no hard feelings. Our family was mad. I stopped being bitter about it after a while, mainly because my dad didn't hold a grudge. I think some of my sisters still do, though. It's just hard to look back at that three-year period, from 1978 to 1980, and see that we won the most regular-season games in that span than anybody else in the NFL. We went 10–6, 10–6, and 11–5. Plus the four playoff wins, two in '78 and two in '79, when we went to the AFC Championship Game twice. We won thirty-five games in three years and we still got fired.

That's when I realized my dad was right when he said, "There are two kinds of coaches in this business. Them that get fired and them that's gonna get fired." That's also when I realized you just do the best you can do, work as hard as you can, because somebody else is going to make the decision about whether what you accomplished was good enough for you to keep your job. You can't brood over it. All you can say is, "If they didn't like it, I'll hopefully go somewhere else."

I will say that my dad and Bud always had a good relationship. We didn't see much of Bud around the team. The only time there was any friction between him and the coaching staff was when we made the playoffs and won playoff games and he didn't want to give us any of the playoff share money. He only wanted to give it to the players.

Nowadays, it's a standard thing around the NFL that teams give playoff shares to coaches as well as to players. But back then, it was up to each individual team, and while other clubs gave the coaches playoff money, Bud didn't. Of course, he had never had to worry about that before because the Oilers won only like sixteen games in the previous five years before Daddy got there.

The first year we were in the playoffs, in 1978, we played in three games, winning two. We should have gotten something like $5,000 each. My dad talked with Bud and also called the league. At some point the league started paying so the owners of the playoff teams weren't responsible. But Bud knew it was only fair to pay the coaches as well. Finally, he gave in, but said, "I wouldn't have paid you if you had lost, but since you won…" It was the same thing the next year. We were fighting for that playoff share the whole time.

Laurie and I went out on New Year's Eve. We walked into a liquor store and who did we see? Ladd Herzeg. We didn't say anything to him. He was buying champagne. We weren't because we knew we didn't have anything to celebrate. It was kind of a sad night all the way around.

One of the oddest things to ever happen to me in football came two or three days later. With Bum being fired, the rest of us on the coaching staff assumed we were fired, too. We all said, "We're going to leave." But Ladd came to us and said, "No, you can't leave. You have a contract. We didn't fire you, we just fired the head coach."

But we all said we didn't want to stay there. We called the league and the response we got was, "You have contracts. We can't do anything about it if they want to make you stay." The next night, Eddie Biles, who had been our defensive coordinator, came to my house.

"I need to talk to you," he said.

"Okay."

"They named me head coach and I want to make you the defensive coordinator."

"Eddie, I can't do that. They fired my head coach, but they also fired my dad. I don't want to stay here."

"Well, it'll be a great opportunity for you. You're young, you know the players and all that."

"Eddie, I can't do that."

The next night, I got another knock on the door. It was Eddie again.

"I need to tell you something," he said while pulling out a piece of paper. "You are under contract with the Houston Oilers, and you cannot leave unless you give up your contract, where nobody's paying you." Then he just read off a statement from that piece of paper that said I had to stay on as a defensive line coach.

"Eddie, you know I'm not staying," I said. He just turned around and walked out.

After that, all of the assistant coaches went into the office. Each of us had to meet with Ladd Herzeg, the general manager. He delivered the same message: "You have to stay or else you will void your next year's contract. You're not getting paid for nothing at all." He was really mad. After hearing a couple of us tell him we wanted to leave, Ladd came out of his office to talk to the entire staff.

"All of you all feel the same way?" he said.

"Yes," we said, almost at the same time. "We don't want to stay here."

He didn't say anything.

Once again, we called the league to see what could be done from that end. Once again, the answer we got was, "Nothing." The only exception was if another team offered any of us a promotion, like a coordinator or head coaching position, we would be able to escape our Oiler contracts and make the upward move.

What Bud Adams and Ladd were basically trying to say was, "Bum was the problem, we needed to get rid of him, and all you guys are good coaches. We just want to get rid of him, name somebody else the head coach, and keep doing what we're doing."

There was also an assumption throughout the organization and Houston and the NFL that Bum already had another job lined up as coach of the New Orleans Saints, because they had just fired Hank Stram. The Oilers were just doing everything they could to discourage us from going with my dad.

It made sense to think that Daddy would end up with the Saints. Their owner, John Mecom, was a Houstonian, and he had come to visit my dad quite a bit when we were getting ready for our playoff games. One time, he gave my dad a stick pin with a diamond on it.

"That's for good luck," John said.

But at that point, Bum had yet to receive any job offer. Things were still up in the air and we were still up in arms. Finally, Joe Bugel, who had been our offensive line coach, left to become offensive coordinator and offensive line coach for the Washington Redskins.

When my dad got the job in New Orleans, he asked me to be the defensive coordinator. After I left, some of the other assistant coaches in Houston went to Ladd Herzeg to reiterate that they didn't want to be there. One of them was King Hill, who had been the offensive coordinator. He was allowed to take the same job in New Orleans. A couple of the other assistants ended up staying because they just weren't forceful enough in trying to get out of their contract.

We also hired Lance VanZandt, who I had worked for at Oklahoma State and KU, as our secondary coach. When he got there, I joked with him, "Hey, now, you've got to get my coffee in the morning instead of me getting yours."

•   •   •

In 1980, the year before we got to New Orleans, the Saints finished 1–15 and had the worst defense in the NFL in every category. They were so bad, it was unbelievable. Everyone in New Orleans started calling them the "Ain'ts." Fans came to games wearing brown paper bags over their heads.

Part of the problem was personnel, obviously. We brought in some younger guys, first- and second-year players, and played them right away. One of them was our running back, George Rogers, who we made the top overall pick of the 1981 draft. The choice was either going to be George or an outside linebacker named Lawrence Taylor. We took George, because we wanted to establish the same foundation with a great back like we did when we made the trade to get Earl Campbell for the number one choice. George had been that kind of player at South Carolina, where he won the Heisman Trophy, just as Earl did at Texas. We had just come from a place where we had won thirty-five games with a great running back, so it seemed like a good pattern to follow.

There were also five or six other really good outside linebackers in the draft, and we felt we would be able to get one of them with our second pick. It turned out, by the time our choice came up, there was only one left: Rickey Jackson from Pittsburgh. LT was a great player and he's in the Hall of Fame, but so was Rickey and he's in the Hall of Fame, too. Sure, we could have had a better defense with both of those guys, but we wouldn't have had any offense at all.

Our first year in New Orleans, we started four rookies on defense and finished eleventh in the league in yards allowed. It was one of our greatest coaching jobs ever. George led the NFL in rushing and was the NFL Offensive Rookie of the Year, but we only had a 4–12 record to show for it. The next year, 1982, was a strike season so we only played nine games and went 4–5. In 1983, the Rams beat us on a forty-two-yard field goal with two seconds left in the final game of the season to give us an 8–8 record. It was tough to come that close to becoming the first Saints team in history to make the playoffs; the best record in the franchise's previous twelve years of its existence was 7–9. That was really disheartening, because we felt we were right on the edge, right on the verge of turning the corner.

Unfortunately, things didn't go the way we wanted with George Rogers. He had some problems off the field, and instead of turning the corner, we went backwards a little in 1984 with a 7–9 finish. After the season, we got rid of George. He ended up with the Washington Redskins and did great for them. But Daddy wanted somebody he could count on, the right kind of person to be his main running back, and we got Earl Campbell back with us from Houston.

The 1985 season started with two losses, but even after three straight wins, we weren't able to get ourselves right. We went on a six-game losing streak. Earl had been through a knee injury and wasn't quite the Earl Campbell he had been in his prime. People were getting mad, and Bum was feeling the brunt of the criticism for everything that was going wrong.

Our fifth loss in that 0–6 stretch was at home, where the Seattle Seahawks beat us, 27–3. As Daddy was walking into the tunnel after the game, a woman in the stands threw a bucket of beer on him. He had walked in before me, so I didn't see it, but he told me about it afterward. It really bothered him more than I had seen anything bother him up to that point.

"I can't do this anymore," he said. "When people throw beer on you over a football game, that just isn't right."

I didn't think much about it because once we got home, we began preparing for our next game at Green Bay, where we lost to the Packers, 38–14. A week later we were at Minnesota, and finally got a win.

Daddy was still really upset over that incident, and once we returned to New Orleans he told Tom Benson, who was in his first season as owner of the Saints, that he was retiring, effective immediately.

"I've coached as long as I want to coach, and now I don't want to coach anymore," he told Tom. "I want to be a rancher."

The rest of us didn't find out about it until well after we got to the facility the next morning. When Bum didn't show up for work, rumors started flying that he had quit. The rest of us tried going through our normal routine of watching film from the day before, but obviously there was nothing routine about that morning. Finally, around 10:00 a.m., Tom Benson told the entire team that Bum had decided to retire. Tom was crying as he spoke to all of the players and coaches, saying what a great guy my dad was. He was very fond of Bum. He didn't want to see him leave.

I was as shocked as everybody else. I was crying right along with Tom. What I didn't realize at the time was that Daddy didn't want to come back to the Superdome again, and our next game after Minnesota was at home against the Rams. He felt humiliated by what had happened three weeks earlier. In his mind, a football game shouldn't cause anyone to react the way that woman did, because we were all trying to do the best we could. That incident pushed him to the point where he felt the job wasn't worth doing anymore. He just wanted to be a cowboy.

He walked away with two years left on his contract, which cost him about $2 million. I don't know many coaches that have ever done that. To his credit, Tom let my dad keep the company car he was driving. Tom also kept him on the team's health insurance, which our family appreciated.

"My job here was to win football games," Daddy said upon announcing his resignation. "And my job here was to provide a winning season. I didn't do that. I'll miss the fans, even the ones that threw beer on me. At least they cared enough to be mad."

Once we all pulled ourselves together, the next question we had was who would be the head coach for the final four games. I got the answer when Tom walked into my office later in the day and said, "I want you to be interim head coach."

"Okay," I told him.

Then, I talked with my dad about it. I was sad, obviously, but I felt Daddy was at peace with his decision. He was ready to move on. He wanted me to take the next step in my coaching career.

"This is a great opportunity for you," he said. "You deserve it. And good luck!"

We beat the Rams, who had a good team that year. That usually happens right after a coaching change. Players play a little bit harder, maybe above the level they had been playing, to make a good impression on the new head coach. But then we lost our final three games to go 5–11 for the season.

I was also the general manager, because that was a job my dad had in addition to being head coach. When the season was over, I had to take care of certain details, organizing the end-of-season physicals with the players and so forth. Some of the coaches on the staff got the impression that because I wasn't fired right after the season, we were all going to be safe for another year. I never thought that. I assumed all along a new general manager would be hired, and when that happened, he was going to bring in his own head coach.

Sure enough, Tom made Jim Finks his new GM. Right after he got the job, Jim called me into his office and said, "Hey, you're gone."

That's how quickly and coldly it happens in this business.

CHAPTER FIVE

FINDING A BUDDY AND A NEW DEFENSE

"I usually try and stay away from contract nego-
tiations. But sometimes they get on high centers.
You know, when you live in the country and you're
drivin' a wagon over them old ruts, all of a sudden
you're on high centers. Your wheels are spinnin'
but you ain't going nowhere."

—Bum Phillips
from *He Ain't No Bum*

I HAD A MEETING WITH AN NFL HEAD COACH AT THE SENIOR Bowl college all-star game in Mobile, Alabama, and he made me an offer to become his defensive coordinator.

I said, "That's great. Okay, I'm coming."

"Good," he said. "We'll work out the salary, but I want you to be the coordinator."

After I got back from Mobile, we had a follow-up call and he said, "I'm gonna fly you in, and we'll get it finished."

I told my wife and kids, "We got a job," and I thought everything was fine. Then things started getting kind of strange. When I called the coach, his secretary told me he wasn't in.

"This is Wade Phillips, and this is my number, have him call me back," I said. He didn't call back. The next day I called again. Same thing, no callback. I called again, and explained to his secretary that the head coach was the one who wanted to talk with me.

She said, "Well, I'm sorry, he's not here."

"Well, just tell him I called and I'm waiting on his call."

I didn't get a callback that time, either.

The next day I called, and when she said he wasn't in for the fourth time, I finally said, "What do you mean he's not there? I'm supposed to take a job there and I'm supposed to talk to him. Where is he?"

"He's out playing golf."

That really chapped me. Finally, he called me back.

"When am I coming in?" I said. "What's going on?"

"Well, there've been some changes. We still want to talk to some other people about the defensive coordinator's job."

"What? You offered me the job; I accepted the job."

"Yeah, but when I got back, things changed."

"Well, then, I'm not coming."

"Well, no, you're still gonna talk to somebody about a contract."

"No, I'm not coming, that's it." And I hung up.

Then I called the GM there and said, "I just want you to know and your owner to know what's going on there. I was offered the job there, accepted the job there, and now your coach is backing out on it. I don't do business that way, I don't think anybody should do business that way, and I'm really upset about it. I want you to tell your owner that, too."

After I hung up, I noticed that the light on our answering machine was blinking. When I pressed play, this is what I heard: "Hey, Wade, Buddy Ryan. I want you to be my coordinator in Philadelphia." Buddy had just become the Eagles' head coach after his great run as defensive coordinator of the Chicago Bears. His "46 defense" had one of the greatest seasons in NFL history as the '85 Bears rolled to a Super Bowl victory over the New England Patriots.

The message was like three or four days old and I'd missed it somehow. Right away, I picked up the phone and dialed the number that Buddy left for me. He was there to take my call.

"Hey, Buddy, it's Wade."

"You want to be the coordinator?"

"Yeah! That'd be great."

"Oh yeah, we'll kick everybody's ass."

"Sounds great."

"Now I want you come in and run my defense."

"Okay. I'd love to learn the 46."

Buddy, who passed away in 2016, was a really personable guy. He was very confident, too, saying things like, "We're gonna kick everybody's ass like we did with the Bears." Except we didn't have the Bears' players, who not only were good but also knew Buddy's scheme well.

We did have some great talent, though, beginning with Hall of Fame defensive end Reggie White. He was one of the two best players I ever coached. The other was Bruce Smith, the Hall of Fame defensive end for the Buffalo Bills.

Reggie was the most powerful guy that I ever coached. For a three-hundred-pound man, he could really move, too. His size and speed allowed him to generate so much power. He could collapse an offensive tackle—meaning he could just push right through his outside shoulder while rushing the passer or even playing the run—better than anybody that played then and has probably played since. If you gave him a running start, you were at a big disadvantage against him.

In 1987, a strike year, Reggie played in only twelve of sixteen games, and still had twenty-one sacks. I know Michael Strahan broke the record with twenty-two-and-a-half sacks in 2001, but he played in all sixteen regular-season games. He also got the benefit of Brett Favre taking a dive in the last game of the season to allow him to break the record. Reggie was like Babe Ruth. He was the man.

With Reggie and all of the pass rushers I coached, I always stressed that you should rush against half a man. You don't want to rush right in the middle of a guy, because now you have to really overpower him. He doesn't have to move his feet. But when you go outside, and you're going against half a man, then he has to move his feet to get in front of you. And Reggie was so powerful that he would collapse that shoulder and run right through the guy.

If they pushed straight back or to the side hard enough, then he would go to his patented "hump" move. For example, if he was rushing from the left end and running at the offensive tackle's right shoulder, he would just sort of swing his right arm and shoulder inside to knock him over. Then, he'd go by him. He would shrug that shoulder, which was the hump, and use the guy's momentum against him.

It was a great experience for me professionally to go with Buddy. He was a brilliant defensive mind. He came up with concepts that were revolutionary at the time. But he didn't explain all of it. He just thought you ought to know it all and be able to teach it all.

After going 5–10–1 and 7–8, we improved to 10–6 and won the NFC East for the first time since the Eagles won it with Dick Vermeil as coach in 1980, but learning the scheme was a real project. With Buddy's defense, everything was multiple. Players also had to audible, adjusting the defense to what they saw as far as formations and movement before the snap. Part of that was because in those days, players couldn't change teams the way they do now, so they had greater familiarity with the terminology because it didn't change very much.

To give an example, when you play a 4–3, you use "Sam"

and "Will" to identify the outside linebackers. "Sam" is on the strong side, because that starts with an *s*. "Will" on the weak side, because that starts with a *w*.

When you put them both on the same side, that's when you get the 46 defense. Now "Will" is going to the strong side, so you can't call him Will anymore.

I asked Buddy, "When you move 'Sam' and 'Will' over to the same side, what do you call them then?"

He said, "Oh, that's Otis and Wilbur." Otis Wilson and Wilbur Marshall were two linebackers he had in Chicago.

"But they're not with us, so we can't call those positions Otis and Wilbur."

"Just teach 'em," Buddy said.

One of the best moves he made was hiring Jeff Fisher, who had been a defensive back for him in Chicago, and had just retired as a player to be his secondary coach. Jeff was really smart and he helped me understand the 46, because he had been a part of it with the Bears and knew it well.

One of the blitzes in Buddy's defense was called the Cheeseburger. I said to Jeff, "Why the hell do you call it the Cheeseburger Blitz?"

Jeff told a story about an outside linebacker the Bears had named Al Harris, who was known as the Destroyer. When a reporter asked Buddy about Harris's nickname, he said, "Destroyer? The only thing I've seen him destroy is a cheeseburger."

That made sense for the Bears. But as I told Jeff, "We don't know who likes cheeseburgers or who doesn't on this team."

Then I asked, "How do you tell the defensive linemen to line up?" I found out was that there really wasn't any system beyond telling them, "In this defense, you line up over the tackle. In this defense, you line up over the guard. In this defense, you…"

It was the same with the coverages. There was no continuity and no way to teach them quickly.

Jeff found out right away that to be able to teach the defense to our players, who had never heard of any of this, we would have to change some things. That's why, when "Will" and "Sam" changed sides, I gave them different names. For instance, when "Will" went to the strong side, he became "Jack." When I told both of them to rush, I could say, "Jack and Sam rushing."

To add to the confusion, in the 46 defense, the strong safety lines up as a weak-side linebacker, but I didn't want to call the strong safety a linebacker. I didn't want to call him the strong safety, because the strong safety lines up on the strong side, not the weak side. Those logistical, terminology things were tough. Also, all the defenses had audibles to change the formation.

Your middle linebacker had to be a genius, because you had a different call for every position. There were twenty formations that the offense could come out in. If they were in the I formation, you played one thing, but if they were in the I slot, you played something else. If they went into motion, you changed it. That's some kind of complicated.

We tried to reduce that to have fewer calls. When they got in the slot, and they got into just regular formation, we didn't change the call all the time. When the offense went into motion, we didn't shift all the time, because the players couldn't do it.

It was the same with coverages. Jeff and I had to come up with a system to teach the players who had who, because the weak safety and strong safety rotated all the time. I had to ask Jeff what the responsibilities were for everybody, because Buddy never said anything about it. When he drew it up on the board, he'd say, "Okay, I want to do the 46 and such and such." He'd draw the defense up against split backs, and he'd walk out.

I said, "Jeff, what if they put the receiver in motion? What if they put the back in motion? What if this happens? We've got to teach all these guys this."

"Yeah, I know, but our guys knew all that."

"But the guys we have here have never even heard of it."

We worked it out. Jeff really helped me there, because he knew the defense. As a first-year coach, he just didn't know how to teach it at that point. He would go on to become a longtime defensive coordinator and head coach in the league.

Buddy hated offense. I've been a defensive coach my whole career and I obviously favor defense, but I've never seen any head coach or defensive coordinator show the kind of ill feelings that Buddy had for the other side of the ball. The offense has a script of the plays it's going to run in practice, usually around twenty-five or thirty, against the "show team" defense, which is made up of backup players playing the part of the opponent.

About eight or ten plays into it, Buddy would go over to the offense in front of everyone and yell, "Hey, I'm tired of looking at this shit. You've got five more plays and then you're done."

The offensive coaches would say, "But, Coach, we've got fifteen more plays we've still got to run."

"I don't care," Buddy said. "I'm tired of looking at this. We're going to defense now."

There were other times, while I was running the show team, he'd come up to me and say, "Hey, run the Cheeseburger Blitz." That isn't how you're supposed to go about business as the show team, because the offense is running its plays thinking that you're going to be following the script and doing what you expect the other team to do against them. I said, "Coach, we're using what we've got on our charts."

"I don't care," Buddy said. "I want to get after them."

We'd run the blitz, they wouldn't be ready for it, and we'd have a bunch of guys in the backfield for what would have been a sack if that was allowed in practice. It wasn't, because you didn't want to get your quarterback hurt, so he wore a red jersey and that meant, "Don't touch."

Offense was just boring for Buddy. He just thought it was a waste of time to practice it. Plus, we had a terrible offense. In 1986, we gave up 104 sacks, a record that will never be broken. The offense in general and the offensive line in particular just drove Buddy crazy. I remember we were ahead in a game in '86, and I turned to him on the sidelines and said, "You know, Buddy, if we run the ball here, we can run the clock out and win the game." At about that time, we threw a pass that got intercepted.

After the game, reporters asked, "Why'd you throw it at the end of the game?"

Buddy, talking about the offensive coaches, said, "Those guys don't know what they're doing." He threw them right under the bus. If you were on offense on Buddy's team, it was brutal.

The only thing Buddy hated more than offense was the Cowboys. In 1987, when NFL players went on strike and there were replacement games that counted, we were one of the teams that decided not to have any of our "real" guys come back until the strike was over—we weren't going to sign anybody but what we called "hey yous." As in, "Hey, you, get off that bar stool and come play for us." We were horrible during the strike and lost all three of the replacement games from weeks four to six. But the Cowboys had some of their best players come back for our game against them in Dallas, such as Hall of Famers Tony Dorsett and Randy White. That really made Buddy mad.

The next time we played the Cowboys at home, we had the ball and were ahead by more than a touchdown with five seconds left. All we had to do was have our quarterback, Randall Cunningham, kneel and the game was over.

During the timeout, Buddy told Randall to fake the kneel-down and throw a pass to Mike Quick. Randall did the fake, threw a deep pass to Mike, who drew an interference penalty at the goal line. Now, there was no time left, but we still had to run a play from the one-yard line because a game can't end on a defensive penalty. We ran it in for a touchdown.

Buddy hated Dallas with a passion. He wanted to stick it to them, no matter what. Thanks to that play, the league put in a rule against faking a kneel-down.

Buddy pretty much let me run his defense because I ran it his way. Well, almost his way. He always wanted me to blitz more than I did, because that was his style. If the other team made a first down, he wanted to blitz them on the next play. But we didn't have the talent he had in Chicago, so it didn't really make sense for us to blitz as much as the Bears did.

Buddy wanted to play man-to-man coverage all the time, because it freed up more people to rush the quarterback. But I got him to put in some zone coverages where you didn't blitz, which I had been successful using in New Orleans. With the Eagles, we had three guys—Reggie White, Clyde Simmons, and Jerome Brown—who could rush the passer like crazy. We also had Mike Golic, who didn't have the talent of the other three but worked hard at getting to the quarterback. My thinking the majority of time was we didn't need to rush more people than our front four. There were a lot of times we needed to be in zone, where we could step back and see the ball and get turnovers. When we started playing more zone, we got a lot of turnovers.

• • •

That whole experience really helped me a lot. I learned what the 46 defense was all about. In fact, some of the 46 defense concepts that I adapted into the 3–4 scheme I run to this day are based on what we used in Philadelphia.

Other lessons I learned from being around Buddy were about things I didn't want to do as defensive coordinator, like making a defense so complicated the players didn't know what to do. That's what happened some of the time in Philadelphia—the players didn't know what to do and people made plays on us because the guys made mistakes. That taught me the importance of making sure players knew their assignments and didn't make assignment errors.

After winning our division in '88, we faced the Bears at Soldier Field in Chicago in a divisional-round playoff game forever known as the Fog Bowl. It was unbelievable—I was sitting in the press box and I couldn't see the field. We had a TV in there, and the camera view from the sideline was a little better, but not much.

As I spoke on the headsets with our coaches standing on the sidelines, they would tell me what they could see and I was telling them what I could see on TV. It was hard to tell what the offense was doing as far as alignment and motion and shifting before the snap, so we mainly used AFC calls, which stands for "automatic front coverage." We just stayed with basic calls for run and pass. If they were in a certain formation, we'd run an eight-man front and drop three guys into coverage. If they weren't, we wouldn't.

The amazing thing was Randall Cunningham threw for more than three hundred yards in that game. But we still lost.

• • •

Buddy had said for a long time that if any of his assistants had a chance to make more money elsewhere, he wouldn't stop them leaving. That was because when he was an assistant with the Jets, he could have gotten a job somewhere else in the league for more money and they wouldn't let him out of his contract.

I didn't think any of us on that coaching staff had a long future in Philadelphia anyway. I remember after a victory we were in the dressing room and the owner of the team, Norman Braman, told Buddy he wanted to speak to the players.

"No, you're not talking to my team," Buddy said. And he didn't let him speak.

I gave a little punch to the assistant coach standing next to me and said, "Hey, we're out of here. Sooner or later, we're not gonna win every game, and we're gonna be gone." But I figured I had a good chance to go to another team before it ever got to that point.

After the 1987 season, Tom Landry called to say he wanted me to come to Dallas to interview for a job on his coaching staff. When I got there, he started asking me all kinds of questions about the 46 defense. We talked for a long time, and I even got up in front of a grease board and diagrammed some things for him. I didn't see it as a risk, like I was giving up some trade secrets, because explaining it and knowing how to coach it are two different things. I was showing him the types of things I would install and how they would work, but I wasn't giving him all of the details of how I taught it and the calls that I made and the all the adjustments and so forth.

Tom's program was starting to go downhill at that point. He told me, "I just need some new ideas. I don't know exactly what I'm looking for, but I'd like somebody that could come in and give us new stuff."

Some of the coaches on his staff had been with him for

about twenty years, including his defensive coordinator, Ernie Stautner, so this would be a difficult change for Tom. But Tom never mentioned anything about me replacing Ernie, so I wanted to make sure he knew exactly where I was coming from in our conversation.

"Hey, I know these guys have been with you, but if I came in, I'd have to be coordinator," I said.

"Well, yeah, I know that," Tom said. "But I just need to get in my mind what we need, whether we need a new spark here or not, and I'm just trying to fit it in my mind."

"Okay."

Later on, Tom called me and said, "Well, I just can't work anything out."

The rest of the story, I'm sad to say, is that Tom kept Ernie as his coordinator and they tried playing the 46 for part of the 1988 season from the stuff he got off the board from me. That really kind of hurt me a little bit, but it hurt Tom a lot more because he didn't know how to adjust to it. The Cowboys went 3–13 that year and their new owner, Jerry Jones, fired Tom and replaced him with Jimmy Johnson.

Around the same time, Dan Reeves, who was coaching the Denver Broncos, fired his defensive coordinator, Joe Collier, and wanted me interview for the job. Joe was a great coach, having headed up the famous Orange Crush defense. My dad had recommended me for the job. It turned out my dad had actually recommended Dan to the Broncos' owner, Pat Bowlen, for the head coaching position after meeting Dan and his family at a golf tournament. The next time Dan saw my dad, he asked him why he had given him the recommendation.

"When I saw you with your family, and knew you were a good family man, I knew you'd be a good coach," Bum told him.

I liked the opportunity in Denver, because I could run a

Daddy and I got a chance to see Wes play at Smoky Hills High School in Aurora, CO.

3–4 defense, which was something they were already running under Joe Collier. One of the first things Dan brought up during the interview was a game between Houston and Dallas, when I was coaching with the Oilers and Dan was a Cowboys assistant. He remembered a fourth-down play the Cowboys had at our twenty-yard line that we had to stop to win the game. We did.

"Why did ya'll play Cover Two down there?" he asked, talking about the fact we had both of our safeties deep so that we would prevent a throw from being completed in the end zone while keeping everything else in front of us. "You played Cover Two four downs in a row. We didn't think you'd be playing it again. Why did you do it?"

"Well, that was our best defense. You always play your best defense when it comes down to one play like that."

"Oh, okay. I like that."

Then the interview got kind of strange.

"I need to ask you some questions," Dan said.

"Okay, Coach."

"Do you talk to your players when they come off the field?"

I thought it was a trick question.

"Well, yeah," I said. "I mean, when they come off the sideline, we'd go over what the last series was, what we're looking for next time, that kind of stuff."

"Okay. Will you play young players?"

I was thinking this was another trick question.

"Well, sure, Coach, we play the best player at every position. If he's young, and he's the best player, we play him, and if he's not, we won't."

"Okay, you've got the job."

We agreed on a salary, shook hands, and that was it.

After I walked out of his office, I went over to talk with Mike Nolan and Charlie Waters, two defensive assistants that Dan had asked me to keep on the staff.

"Mike, Charlie, I just had the strangest interview ever," I said. "Dan asked me if I talk to the players when they come off the sideline."

They started laughing, then explained that Joe Collier had so many different defenses, if there was a bad play, he just wouldn't call that defense again so there was no reason to discuss what went wrong with the players. Joe also wouldn't play young players because his defense was so complicated they needed a few years before they would know what to do.

We ended up cutting a lot of guys who knew how to play Joe Collier's defense but weren't good fits for the scheme I was using. The media made a big deal about it, calling it the "Massacre of Fort Collins," because we held our training camp in Fort Collins, Colorado. They also weren't really good players. We did have a couple of key pieces already there in safety Dennis Smith and linebacker Karl Mecklenburg.

Dan was a lot more volatile than I thought he was. You don't know people until you get into the game with them, and what I found out about Dan was that he'd get mad at things during a game. If the defense didn't make a stop, he'd be really upset.

He was tough on assistant coaches overall. If players didn't do something right, it was the coaches' fault—the position coach and the coordinator on that side of the ball. The Seahawks were in the AFC West at the time, so the Broncos faced them twice a year. When I got there, one of the things Dan kept talking about was the Seahawks making thirty-two first downs against his defense the year before.

"Thirty-two!" Dan would tell me, over and over, making sure I wouldn't forget.

Each year for the Senior Bowl college all-star game in Mobile, Alabama—a showcase for top draft prospects—NFL coaching staffs guide North and South all-star squads. In '89 our Broncos staff had the North. You only play certain parts of your offense and defense, very basic stuff, because you don't want to show everybody what you're doing. On the first drive of the game, the South started marching down the field—first down, first down, first down.

Now, I didn't realize how much of a competitor Dan was, and he was getting mad. I mean, the veins were sticking out of his neck. Even though it was just an all-star game and wouldn't count against his NFL coaching record, Dan didn't want to get beat. Ever. You just had to know him. That's what made him a good coach. After the South made its third or fourth first down, I walked by Dan on the sidelines and said to him, "Coach, how am I doing so far?"

The rest of the coaches couldn't believe I said that, but even though Dan was mad, he allowed himself to laugh. We opened the season against Kansas City, and our first touchdown came on a thirty-four-yard interception return by Tyrone Braxton.

After that, I said, "How we doin' so far, Coach?"

"Great!"

We finished with an 11–5 record and led the league in least points given up. People forgot about the "massacre" pretty fast. We also went to the Super Bowl, where we lost to San Francisco, 55–10.

John Elway, our Hall of Fame quarterback who is now the Broncos' executive vice president of football operations, was horrible. The offense was horrible. The defense was bad, too.

What I found out is the Super Bowl's an even bigger game than you think, because if they make a play on you, it seems bigger than anything that's ever happened to you. When you make a play, you're elated and you think it's the greatest thing ever. But if they make a play, you can't let that affect you on the next play.

I'll never forget, the first play of the game against San Francisco, Elway dropped back to pass and threw an out route. The receiver was open…and the ball hit the ground about eight yards in front of him. I remember everybody on the sideline going, "Oh my gosh!" The whole team treated it as the biggest letdown ever. John didn't complete that pass, and the whole game went like that. I learned that you've got to control your emotions a lot more than you do in a regular game, especially when something goes wrong.

CHAPTER SIX

THE MUSIC CITY MISTAKE

"I consider kickers to be football players. In a
10–7 ballgame, one of 'em is the difference."

—Bum Phillips
from *He Ain't No Bum*

SOMETIMES, YOU JUST WEAR OUT YOUR WELCOME AS A HEAD coach, and I think that was the case with Dan Reeves in Denver. He had taken the team to three Super Bowls, including the one in my first year with the Broncos—their third in a four-year span. He also had taken them to the AFC Championship Game, when we got beat by Buffalo. In spite of his success, Dan was fired after our 8–8 finish in 1992, my fourth season in Denver.

The Broncos wanted to replace him with Mike Shanahan, who was the 49ers' offensive coordinator at the time, but he turned them down. Mike had been an offensive assistant with Denver until Dan fired him after only two seasons, but he just didn't feel that was the right time to take the job.

John Beake, the general manager, walked in my office and said, "We want you to be the head coach. Here's the contract." I didn't hesitate to sign it, because I wanted to be a head coach and this was my opportunity. I didn't have an agent and I know

I didn't do myself any favors by taking what was a pretty low deal by NFL head-coaching standards. All I really did was make it easier for the Broncos to fire me, because it wasn't going to cost them all that much to walk away from that contract. But the only thing I cared about was the chance to become a head coach on a full-time basis rather than the interim label I had in New Orleans.

My first season, we went 9–7 and reached the playoffs, where we lost to the Los Angeles Raiders 42–24 in the wild card round. My second year, we went 7–9, ending my first full-time head coaching opportunity—I was fired right after the season. I was proud of the fact that in the first year we made a trade with Minnesota for offensive tackle Gary Zimmerman, who would go on to the Pro Football Hall of Fame. In the second year, we used a seventh-round draft pick to select Tom Nalen, who would go onto become one of the top centers in the NFL. Right after that draft, I was the one who placed a phone call to Rod Smith to sign him as a rookie free agent. He would go on to become the Broncos' career leader in receptions, receiving yards, and receiving touchdowns.

That second year, our owner, Pat Bowlen, was having some money issues. It got so bad that he sold the suites he used at Mile High Stadium just to get some cash. Because of Pat's financial difficulties, we were letting some good players go and not signing the best free agents. John Elway missed two games with an injury that season, and we lost both of them.

I also let my defensive assistant coaches talk me into switching from a 3–4 to a 4–3. I should have never done that, because I'm better at running a 3–4 and we just weren't as good on defense as we had been. But two of my coaches, Charlie Waters and John Paul Young, both of whom had backgrounds with the 4–3, thought we ought to make the switch because it was better

Taking a little postgame victory walk with Wes at Mile High Stadium.

suited to our personnel. We went into that season a little short of linebackers, which can be a problem when you're playing a 3–4 because that defense is predicated on having a lot of depth at linebacker. I also felt like we had better defensive linemen, another factor in favor of using the 4–3. I'm always about doing what's best for your players, but we just didn't play it well.

The 49ers would win the Super Bowl that year, making Mike Shanahan a hot coaching commodity. The Broncos had wanted him in the first place, and once they saw how well he did with the 49ers' offense, they wanted him even more this time. I couldn't blame them. Mike's a really good coach. Three seasons after he took the job, the Broncos would win the first of back-to-back Super Bowls.

After the 1994 season, the Bills let go of their defensive coordinator, Walt Corey, and wanted me to take his place on the staff of their Hall of Fame head coach, Marv Levy. The main reason for their interest was how well our defense had played against them in that 1991 AFC Championship Game in Buffalo when I was the Broncos' defensive coordinator. That was one of the first things John told me when he offered me the job.

The Bills won 10–7 but their offense, which was one of the most explosive in the league, scored only three points. They had Jim Kelly at quarterback, running that no-huddle attack with fellow future Hall of Famers Thurman Thomas at running back and Andre Reed and James Lofton at wide receiver. Yet their only touchdown came on Carlton Bailey's 11-yard return of an interception of an Elway pass. They finished with only 213 total yards (including a mere 109 through the air) to our 304, and had only twelve first downs to our twenty.

We had a pretty good game plan to take away some of the things the Bills' offense did. For instance, every time they split Thurman Thomas out from the backfield, we blitzed one of our safeties, usually Dennis Smith, and that gave them real problems because there was no one in the backfield to block him. What the Bills did was pick you apart by calling plays at the line of scrimmage, based on what Jim Kelly and his receivers and linemen saw from your alignment.

With great quarterbacks and great offenses, you've got to come up with some things they haven't seen, so we changed up our coverages a little bit and did some disguising—we showed a coverage before the snap that we wanted them to think we were playing and then changed to the actual coverage we were going to play right after the snap. We just mixed them up a little bit. By us bringing an extra pass rusher a lot of the time, they didn't have as much protection as they normally would and we were able to pressure Jim to throw the ball faster than he wanted to. We had a really talented defense too, so that was a big part of it.

The Bills went 10–6 and made the playoffs in each of my

first two years in Buffalo. They were starting to decline a bit from the team that made four Super Bowls in a row, but the defense had some good players, such as Bruce Smith, one of the best players I ever coached besides Reggie White.

They had two very different playing styles. Reggie was all about power, while Bruce was a great athlete. He could have played tight end or whatever. In fact, he played tight end in practice sometimes. He was the kind of guy that made you say, "Wow!" Bruce was so quick and so athletic. What he did really well was just bend, getting low enough that even as tall as he was at six foot four, he could beat a guy around the corner before the guy could get his feet in front of him. He could just go under their hands. They'd try punching at him and he'd duck and go around them. It was like watching an Olympic runner going around the curve perfectly and then running down the straightaway right to the quarterback.

He also had a great feel for what offensive tackles tried to do to block him. If they overset, lining up with an eye toward getting in front of him outside, then he could beat them inside. But he was the best ever at just rushing around the outside corner. He was the most consistent, too. He was in tremendous shape all the time. A lot of that was because the Bills had one of the all-time greatest strength and conditioning coaches in Rusty Jones, who had all of the players following diets and training that emphasized lowering body fat. The players would actually compete with each other to come to training camp with the lowest body fat.

The amazing thing with Bruce, though, was that he almost never practiced in camp. It seemed like he was recovering from an operation every year, so he was always kept out of practice. One year he didn't practice the whole camp, except for some individual drills, and didn't take one snap in the preseason. We played the Giants in the first game of the 1996 regular season, and Bruce wound up being on the field for eighty-five plays. The eighty-fifth came in overtime, when he sacked the quarterback and forced a fumble that we recovered to set up the winning field goal.

I always tell that story to other players, because the message is that you can be in shape if you want to. Even though he didn't practice or play in any preseason games, he'd be on the Stairmaster and the treadmill forever. He really worked harder than people thought.

I think Bruce wanted to make everybody think that everything he did was natural, but he worked at everything he did. He'd come in on Tuesdays, the players' day off, and study the guy that he was going to face, deciding what he was going to do against him. Then he'd get two sacks in the game, and afterward he'd say, "I just beat the guy."

Bruce was so smart, too. A lot of the defensive linemen just try to whip the guy in front of them. But Bruce knew the game. He could recognize formations.

Bruce would also play the run. A lot of those guys that had all those sacks over the years didn't play the run. Bruce did. We utilized his quickness to let him move a lot, let him stunt inside and outside. Phil Hansen, our other defensive end, was a really good player, but he didn't have Bruce's talent, so we tied him down more and pretty much kept him over the tight end.

The Bills also had some guys on the decline, so we went out and got some help. One of our biggest additions the first year I was there was Bryce Paup, a free agent outside linebacker from the Green Bay Packers. The following season, we brought in Chris Spielman, who had established himself as a top inside linebacker with the Detroit Lions.

• • •

We started to lose some of the major pieces of those Super Bowl teams when Jim Kelly and our center, Kent Hull, retired after the 1996 season. We didn't have anyone who came close to Kelly's ability at quarterback, so we finished 6–10 in 1997. Marv Levy retired at the end of the year and a short while later, John Butler, the general manager, walked up to me and said, "I want you to be the head coach." I said, "That'd be great." He said they would be interviewing some other people, but he thought I was the best man for the job.

After that, John called me at home and said Ralph Wilson, the Bills' owner, was going to give me a call to offer me the job. This time, I was determined to do a better job of negotiating than I had done with the Broncos.

When Ralph told me what he wanted to pay me, I said, "No, I'm not going to take the job for that."

"What?"

"Ralph, I'm almost making that right now."

After my second year as defensive coordinator, which was when my original contract was about to expire, there had been a rumor the Miami Dolphins wanted to hire me as their defensive coordinator. I don't know where it started; maybe I started it. Anyway, I hired an agent and told him I wanted the Bills to pay for my move from the house we were renting to one we had bought and also make me the highest-paid defensive coach in the league. I got both.

Next we tried to figure out a number that would work for both of us. Ralph wouldn't talk to my agent, so I had to do this one on my own. The Indianapolis Colts had just hired Jim

Mora to be their head coach, so Ralph said, "Well, would you take that?"

"Yeah, I'd take that."

"Okay, three-year deal, but no raises. Just a flat number for three years."

Ralph gave me the additional title of vice president of football operations. He wanted me to answer directly to him rather than the GM. That wasn't a problem with John. We worked great together on everything—picking the roster, drafting players, signing free agents.

Part of the reason I thought we lost in '96 was because we didn't have a quarterback. So one of the first things I said after taking the job was, "We've got to get a quarterback."

First, we signed Doug Flutie, who after an unsuccessful start to his career in the NFL went on to become the greatest player in the history of the Canadian Football League. A.J. Smith, who was our director of pro personnel, loved Flutie. When he said he thought we could get him from the CFL, I said, "Let's get him."

I didn't know that much about Doug, other than the fact he was only five foot ten and that he had originally come into the NFL after winning the Heisman Trophy and making a miracle Hail Mary pass that allowed Boston College to upset the University of Miami. The Chicago Bears tried to play him as soon as he got there as a rookie in 1985, but they didn't have an offense that fit his skills as a smaller guy who runs around the pocket to make plays. Then he went up to Canada and proved he was a really good player.

We also traded first- and fourth-round draft picks to the Jacksonville Jaguars for Rob Johnson. Rob had been a backup in Jacksonville for three seasons, appearing in only eight games and making only one start. The one start was pretty good. He completed twenty-two of twenty-eight passes for 344 yards and two touchdowns, with two interceptions. We gave up a lot to get him, but we looked at the film and the guy could spin the ball.

I was just trying to get as many quarterbacks as we could get to find somebody who could play, but the media started talking about us having a quarterback controversy. They said we had a divided locker room, with some the older guys wanting Doug to start and the younger guys being behind Rob. I didn't think it was that big of a deal, but the media obviously did.

The owner of the team, Ralph Wilson, picked a side as well after we played Washington in our last preseason game that summer. Flutie played and drove us the length of the field at the end of the game for the winning points. Afterward, Ralph came up to me in the training room, with lots of people around us, and said, "This Flutie, we've got to get rid of him. He can't play!"

"Mr. Wilson, he took us on a ninety-nine-yard drive for a touchdown to win the game," I said.

"I don't care, I don't care. He ran the ball, he was running with it sometimes."

"But that's what it takes. That's the great thing about him. He can make plays whether he's throwing it or running with it or pitching it out to somebody or anything."

"Oh, I don't like him."

We began the season 0–3 with Rob as our starter, but he wasn't able to stay healthy. After watching Doug lead us to a big division road win against Indianapolis to get us to 3–2, Ralph said, "I love that Flutie! I love him!" You just never knew what you were going to get with Ralph, which I actually thought was kind of fun at times.

We ended up with a 10–6 record and made the playoffs in my first year as the Bills' head coach. Doug started in a wild card playoff game at Miami that we lost, 24–7. I thought we were in good shape at quarterback in spite of the loss, because Flutie was older and Rob still looked like someone we could develop for the future. Doug also was limited in some ways because of his lack of height, but he was outstanding in others.

One way he was exciting was his running. He could make plays with his feet that no one else could make. He also had great instincts and a feel for what defenses were doing and how to take advantage of them. In one of his first games with the Bills, he started running toward our sidelines. He was about five or six yards past the line of scrimmage when he suddenly pitched the ball, it seemed, right to me as I was standing on the sidelines. I'm thinking, *What's he doing?*

All of a sudden, Thurman Thomas came running down the sidelines and he grabbed the ball and kept running for what turned out to be a twenty-yard lateral. You just didn't see players

My reaction to Doug Flutie's touchdown run that allowed the Bills to beat Jacksonville.

do things like that. You still don't. It was a gift that Doug had, plus tremendous confidence in his ability to do it.

Doug's running proved to be the difference in our sixth game of that season at home against Jacksonville. There was a lot riding on it, including the future of the Bills in Buffalo. The Bills were trying to raise money from local businesses to help fund a big renovation of what was then called Ralph Wilson Stadium. People needed a reason to be excited, and Doug gave it to them when we had the ball on the Jaguars' one-yard line with eighteen seconds left.

We went with three wide receivers, and the call was that if Doug had a chance to run it up the middle for the score himself he would. If he didn't think he'd make it, he'd hand it to the running back, who would run it up the middle for the score. And if he saw that there were too many people in the box, he would bootleg it, which was what he did. He just ran to his left as fast as he could and got into the corner of the end zone to give us a 17–16 win.

The place went crazy and the business folks started writing big checks to help pay for the renovation. It's no stretch to say that Doug had a lot to do with the Bills staying in Buffalo.

Doug was our starter in 1999. We were 10–5 and already had a playoff spot clinched before the final game of the season, which was at home against the Colts, so we decided to rest Doug and start Rob. Rob ended up having his best game ever. He threw for 287 yards and a couple of touchdowns to lead us to a 31–6 win.

The next day, Ralph Wilson called our GM, John Butler, to tell him he wanted Rob to start our wild card playoff game at Tennessee. It wasn't a bad idea, considering the Titans were unbeaten at home and won all their games there by big scores. We had just played one of our best games of the whole season, and Rob played tremendously. Plus, if we weren't playing well, Flutie could come in and give us a spark.

Rob was talented when it came to throwing the ball—he had arm talent. But he was a perfectionist. Everything had to be perfect—the route, the protection. If everything wasn't perfect, he would hold the ball, and he got sacked a lot because of that. If you watched him at practice, he was a better passer than Doug, and under some circumstances a better player. If you watched Rob in seven-on-seven, a pure passing drill with no one rushing the quarterback, he would always look great. But under other circumstances, he wasn't as good a player as Doug.

Part of what made Doug such a good player was that he was a great competitor. I know he was really upset about the decision to go with Rob, although he didn't say anything directly to me. I just said, "Hey, this is what we're gonna do and go from there. You may have the opportunity to play, you may not. We'll just see." I don't blame Doug for being mad. He had played really well. I did think he was worn down physically at the end of the season, which was part of why we didn't play him in that Indianapolis game. We wanted him fresher, and then the other guy did so well that circumstances changed.

You've got to be honest with any player. You let them know how it is, whether they like it or they don't like it. That's the way you coach. What you don't say is, "Well, the owner told me to play the other guy, and I'm playing him because of that," or anything like that. When you present something as a coach, you have to present as, "Here's what we're doing as a team," because you want the player to know that it's everyone's job to do everything possible to make the plan work, regardless of how anyone feels about it.

I wasn't worried about the players on the team who were in Doug's corner being angry about the switch. If you're coming off a big win like we were, I don't think that happens. If it's after a loss, I think it's different. Once you lose and there's a change, then all hell can break loose.

That decision was looking pretty good when Rob drove us down to set up what we all thought was the winning field goal from forty-one yards by Steve Christie with sixteen seconds left. We still had a kickoff to cover, but everything seemed to be in our favor up until that point. Then, Bruce DeHaven, our special-teams coach who had been with the Bills a long time, came up to me and said, "You want to kick it deep?"

"Yeah," I said.

He came up with another suggestion. "Why don't we bloop kick it?"

"Oh, okay."

A bloop kick is higher and shorter than a regular kickoff, and you do it to take more time off the clock than kicking it through the end zone and putting the other team on the twenty-yard line (which now has been moved to the twenty-five). Now I thought he was going to have Steve bloop it outside the numbers, where you'd have them pinned as far as the coverage could prevent the returner from going up the field or toward the middle. Even if the ball goes out of bounds, and you get a penalty that gives the other team good field position, so what? They would still have only sixteen seconds to score.

But what we did was completely the opposite, because we blooped it down the middle. Lorenzo Neal caught Steve's kick and handed off to Frank Wycheck, who threw the ball across the field to Kevin Dyson who ran down the sidelines seventy-five yards for a touchdown. The officials said it was a legal lateral, but I was standing right across from where Wycheck threw the ball and I know it was an illegal forward pass.

I said, "Well, they're going to call it back, because we've got instant replay." In fact, I was so sure they would overturn it, I was thinking ahead to the clock needing to be reset to when the penalty occurred. I figured that would still only leave them enough time for one play, so we needed to get our prevent defense ready.

When the official came back and said, "The ruling on the field stands," I just lost it. I took off my headset and threw it on the ground. All the air just went out of me.

"Oh, God," was the only thing I could say.

It was close, I'll say that much. I think they just didn't want to overrule it, especially in a hostile environment. They probably thought they would have gotten lynched there.

In Tennessee, the play is forever known as the Music City Miracle. I'll always remember it as the Music City Mistake.

I will say it was also a bad plan on our part to bloop the ball in the middle, and have all of our coverage guys go to the middle of the field. That was my fault. You have to have a plan for those situations, and I just didn't think we had a good plan. We weren't ready for that play. They did a better job of preparing for it than we did. Part of that fell on Bruce, but most of it fell on me for not telling him exactly what I wanted him to do. We also hadn't really worked on blooping a kick to the outside.

I was sick for everybody. I thought we fought hard to win the game, but ended up losing it because of two bad plays on special teams. Right before the half, the Titans had missed a field goal, but we were called for defensive holding, they got to kick it again, and made it. Take away that penalty, and we wouldn't have even had to go down for those three points at the end of the game.

Afterward, I spoke with my dad on the phone and he just asked me, "Why did ya'll kick it short down the middle?"

"Well, I didn't know we were going to do that," I said.

The return was a miscommunication between Bruce and me. I really felt that we let the team down by not having a better plan for the situation. I regret not telling Bruce, who passed away in 2016, specifically want I wanted. In the end, the Music City Mistake was mine.

That spring, our coaching staff sat down with one of the NFL officiating crews that annually go around to each team in the league to review all the new rules. We met in our staff meeting room where they would be able to show us video of certain plays from the previous season to explain why calls were or weren't made and how they would be officiated under the new rules.

All of a sudden, one of the first plays to appear on the screen was the Music City Mistake. They didn't just show the play, but they also said it was an example of "why we've got good officiating" in the NFL. I couldn't believe it. None of us could. There they were, in the building of the team that was on the wrong end of that whole deal, talking with the coaching staff with emotional wounds that were still pretty raw, and they're trying to tell us what a great job the officials did on *that* play? Of all of the hundreds of plays to choose from, they couldn't come up with a different one to show us?

That really made me mad. Every coach in that room was fuming. As far as I was concerned, our meeting was over.

"Turn it off!" I said. "We don't want to see that. First of all, it's wrong. And for you to sit there and say it's right is wrong. You need to get out of here right now."

They did. Quietly.

• • •

We went 8–8 the following year. With a couple of games left, Ralph fired John Butler, so he was going to be hiring a new GM. I knew that meant there was a very good chance that GM would want to hire his own head coach.

Sure enough, rumors started flying that Ralph was going to fire me because he traveled with the team to our final game in Seattle, something he rarely did. We beat the heck out of the Seahawks, 42–23. We finished with 579 yards of offense, 3 yards short of an all-time team record set in 1991. In fact, if we hadn't had Doug kneel down at the end of the game, losing a few yards in the process, we would have set the record.

Ralph didn't fire us after the game, but the rumors were still going around. After we got back to Buffalo, I went down to his winter home in West Palm Beach for the annual postseason meeting that he has with his coach. We talked about a lot of stuff. One of them was the quarterback.

"We're gonna keep one of them," Ralph said. "Which one would you keep?"

"Doug."

I'm pretty sure that wasn't the answer he was looking for, but that was how I felt.

Then he talked about the coaches.

"I don't like this one, I don't like that one," Ralph said, going through the whole staff. We spent some time talking about Ronnie Jones, who had had a rough time with our special teams.

"Well, I'm changing his job," I said. "I'm gonna keep him, he's a good coach. He's just not the special-teams coach that we need. I'll get another special team's coach, and let him help out on defense."

That was the way we left things when I headed back to Buffalo. But I kept hearing the rumors that I was going to lose my job, so I called him to find out if they were true.

"Are you gonna fire me, or what's going on here?" I asked.

"Oh, you're my coach," he said.

"Well, okay."

Jim Overdorf, a member of the front-office staff, was with me and heard the whole conversation.

The rumors that I was going to be fired wouldn't stop, so right before I was supposed to fly to San Francisco for the East-West college all-star game, I called Ralph and I said, "Look, I normally go to the East-West game, should I take this trip?"

"Just do what you normally do."

"Oh, okay, but I'm hearing rumors."

"Go ahead and do what you normally do."

I went to the East-West game. As soon as I got into my hotel room, I got a phone call.

"Wade, this is Ralph." He was mad. He wasn't talking. He was hollering. "I told you to fire that guy!"

"What guy?"

"That Jones guy! You were supposed to fire him."

"No, sir, we talked about that. I told you what I was gonna do."

"Well, I don't care. You know what I wanted you to do."

"But we talked about him, we talked about several other coaches. Look, if you want to fire all my coaches, then you ought to just fire me."

"Okay, you're fired. I'm calling the PR guy right now to make the announcement."

That was it. He hung up the phone.

The worst was yet to come. Ralph tried not to pay me, saying that I had quit and breached my contract. But I knew he had fired me, because he said it. Every newspaper in the country reported it that way.

I had to file a grievance with the league. We had a hearing

with an arbitrator that Ralph was supposed to attend the day after the draft. But Ralph said he couldn't make it because he was sick. When I found out he'd attended the draft, I called the league office and said, "This is a bunch of you know what."

Two weeks later, we finally had the hearing in Buffalo. I had a lawyer, and that cost me a lot of money. But I knew I would win because what Ralph was saying was untrue. During the arbitration, he was asked about the new GM he had hired, Tom Donahoe.

"When did you hire him?" Ralph was asked.

"I hired him right after I fired Wade."

That was in the transcript. As soon as I heard that, I thought, *This is over.*

Six months went by and there was still no word from the arbitrator. Meanwhile, I wasn't getting paid, so I kept calling the league. They kept telling me, "The arbitrator hasn't made his final ruling." I was getting upset with the league, and the league lawyer said, "Well, I think everything's going to work out alright."

"But I'm sitting around not getting paid. My dad was in the league; I've been in the league a long time. We've stood by the NFL. I could have gone to the USFL as a head coach, but I didn't do that. I feel like I've done right by the league, and you need to get something done for me."

My lawyer kept saying, "Don't keep pushing them, or they'll get mad and rule against you." Keep in mind, the arbitrator worked for the league, which meant he worked for Ralph and the rest of the owners.

Finally, they sent the ruling to both of us, saying Ralph owed me all of the back pay, but with no interest and no lawyer's fees, which came out to about $50,000. I was just happy it was over.

• • •

After being fired, I went to Washington to interview with Marty Schottenheimer to become the Redskins' defensive coordinator. I thought it would be a good-paying job, with an owner like Daniel Snyder who was known for paying his coaches well. I talked with Marty about the 3–4, which he didn't have a background in. He was a 4–3 guy. I talked with him for about three hours. Afterward, he told me I had the job.

Then somebody called me and said, "Have you seen the Washington paper?"

"No."

"Well, you better read that."

In the paper, there was a quote from Marty saying, "I'm deciding between Wade and my brother, Kurt, to see which one's the best guy for the job." Right away, I called Marty and said, "What are you talking about in this article?"

He started hemming and hawing.

"You're using me so you can say your brother's a better defensive coach than I am."

He wound up hiring his brother, although I will say that Kurt Schottenheimer is a very good coach.

CHAPTER SEVEN

WITH AMERICA'S TEAM, IT'S ALWAYS SUPER BOWL OR BUST

"I always thought I could coach. I just thought people were poor judges of good coaches."

—Bum Phillips
from *He Ain't No Bum*

AFTER FALLING SHORT WITH THE REDSKINS, I INTERVIEWED FOR the head coaching job with the Houston Texans. They ended up hiring Dom Capers.

I spent the 2001 season out of football. It wasn't so bad, because our son, Wesley, was a senior on the football team at the University of Texas El Paso. We moved to Austin, which wasn't too far from El Paso, and we got to go to all of his home games and some of the ones on the road. We also have a daughter, Tracy, who is an actress, dancer, and choreographer living in Southern California.

After a year away from football, I had two opportunities to become a defensive coordinator in 2002. One was with the New York Giants, the other with the Atlanta Falcons.

My agent set up conversations with Jim Fassel, the Giants' head coach at the time and my offensive coordinator when I

Celebrating Dad's birthday with Wes at the University of Texas at El Paso.

was head coach of the Broncos, and with Dan Reeves, who was coaching the Falcons.

Finally, my agent said to me, "I think I can get you the same money from either one. Where would you want to go?"

"I'm from the South," I said. "I feel like the Giants have the better defense going in. They have the better players. But I'd rather go to Atlanta, because I'm more of a Southern type of guy. And I had worked for Dan before and thought he was a great coach."

I wound up going to the Falcons. I can't stress enough how much I appreciated Dan. Most of the time, when somebody gets fired and a coordinator takes his place, as I did in Denver, the head coach who lost his job is not happy with you. A lot of people are telling him, "Hey, he stabbed you in the back to get your job." Here's Dan, hiring me the very next chance he had as a head coach. A lot of coaches wouldn't do that.

In coaching, once you're fired, it's not your job anymore. That's why I've never felt bad about taking someone's place or someone taking my place. They weren't trying to get my job. It just happened. They got the opportunity.

The first year in Atlanta was tremendous. After going 9–6 and making the postseason, we handed the Green Bay Packers their first playoff loss at home 27–7. That was a pretty phenomenal victory. The following week, we lost at home to Philadelphia, 20–6. We played well in that one, too. But our quarterback, Michael Vick, had a fifty-yard touchdown run called back.

The second year, Michael broke his leg in the preseason and we didn't have a good enough backup. We didn't play well overall as a team, but I think the lack of quality depth behind Michael was really the key factor. Late in the season, Dan was hearing the rumors that our owner, Arthur Blank, wanted to fire him. So he walked into Arthur's office and said, "I heard I might be fired at the end of the season. Is that true?"

"Yes," Arthur said.

"Okay, then I'm leaving."

With three games left, Dan was gone, and for the second time in my career I was named interim coach. We won the last two, mainly because Michael Vick came back from his injury. Between Michael and our running back, Warrick Dunn, we finished fourth in the NFL in rushing offense.

I interviewed to become the full-time head coach and thought I did well. But having been through the interim experience in New Orleans, I knew I wasn't going to get it. You really don't have a chance under those circumstances. It's not your team. Maybe it's half of your team if you coached the defense.

Arthur Blank did tell me that Warrick and several other players told him they wanted me as the coach, which is really the kiss of death because most team owners don't think players are supposed to like their coach. They'd rather have players fear the coach. They think that's what coaching is—you're the boss and everybody else is subservient, so to speak.

It's a natural thing. It's happened forever in coaching. It happened to my dad when he was an assistant at SMU. A bunch of players got together and sent a Western Union telegram to the school president to try to get him to be the head coach. It didn't work.

When I left, I told Arthur and the general manager, Rich McKay, "This team is a gold mine. You've got a great quarterback in Michael Vick. You've got one of the league's best rushing offenses with Warrick and Michael."

Ironically, the Falcons ended up hiring Jim Mora Jr. as their head coach. I say ironically, because Jim Mora Sr. had replaced me in New Orleans.

I wasn't out of work long when I got a call from A.J. Smith, now the Chargers' GM. We got along well from our

With Tracy and Wes and some key lime pie for Christmas in Atlanta.

time together in Buffalo. He wanted me to interview with the head coach, Marty Schottenheimer, to become his defensive coordinator.

"I'm not gonna do that," I said. "I've been through this before with Marty, and I am not gonna go out there and have him tell me he's going to hire his brother again."

"That's not going to happen," Smith said. "I've already talked to Dean Spanos, the owner, and he said we're not hiring anyone in the family. That's part of our policy." At least where coaches were concerned—the Spanoses had a bunch of their family members working for the team.

I took A.J. at his word and flew to San Diego. Marty interviewed me for about three hours, just as he had in Washington. Nobody else ever went that long with me, because I didn't have to interview for a lot of jobs. Either they want you or they don't. I spent much of that time with Marty standing in front of a grease board, showing him the 3–4 defense, which he still didn't have a great feel for. Once again, he asked a million questions, because Marty had been playing a 4–3 defense.

I can't say why he would've been okay with making the switch to the 3–4. I didn't know all that was going on behind the scenes, if A.J. was pulling the strings or whatever, but Marty said that if he did hire me, he wanted me to run my defense.

When we finished, he said, "Okay, that was good. We've got some other people to talk to."

"Well, I've got some other people to talk to."

"That's fine. After we talk to those other people, something may or may not come up."

"That's fine. And if I get something before that, I may take it."

I got to the airport and as I was waiting for my plane, I got a call.

"Wade, this is Marty."

"Yeah, Marty."

"We want to offer you the job."

"Okay, I'll take it."

Working for Marty Schottenheimer in 2004 put me in the strangest situation I've ever been in during my career. You talk about having complete autonomy. Every once in a while, he'd say, "Well, I don't like so and so playing, I think so and so is better."

I'd say, "No, well, I think so and so is good enough, and he should be starting." And that was it. He let me pick all of the defensive players. I don't know if he was under orders never to say anything to me or what, but it was a different deal.

At our very first meeting as a coaching staff, Marty said, "I don't care what your contract says, if we don't win this year, we're all getting fired." Having just signed a three-year deal, I said to myself, "Okay, that was an interesting first meeting."

The way Marty and A.J. communicated was also interesting. They just didn't seem to be on the same page.

Marty was a real showman and very good at motivating the team. He was always asking me, "What should I talk to the team about? What do you think they would like to hear?" He would often blow the whistle and call the team up during practice to talk to them. After a player made a play and came to the sideline during a game, Marty would make sure to greet him, putting both arms around his shoulders and start talking to him like he was telling him something really important even if it was just, "Good job on that play."

Part of the reason I took the job was because the Chargers were the worst team in football the year before they hired me, which was why they had the top pick of the draft. I had been successful with teams that weren't good before, but this was the biggest challenge ever. They had a good offense. LaDainian Tomlinson was at running back with Michael Turner backing him up. Drew Brees was at quarterback, with Philip Rivers backing him up. But our defense wasn't good at all.

We wound up going 12–4, reversing the 2003 record of 4–12, and we were able to make the defense a lot better. We lost a wild card playoff game against the New York Jets. We went 9–7 the following season and just missed the playoffs. Drew ended up hurting his shoulder at the end of the year. After the season, he became a free agent, which began the Philip Rivers era in San Diego.

The Miami Dolphins had a chance to sign Drew, but didn't trust that his shoulder would ever heal right. The Saints took a chance on him, which ended up being one of the best gambles any team took on a player.

We had a league-best 14–2 record in our third season in San Diego. This time we lost in the divisional round of the playoffs to New England, but that season helped me get a head coaching job with the Dallas Cowboys. The Miami Dolphins hired our offensive coordinator, Cam Cameron, to be their head coach.

You would think with a record like that Marty would have been able to keep his job. But there was some sort of disagreement between him and A.J. that finally came to a head, and Norv Turner wound up replacing Marty as head coach.

Of course, Dallas is a big job. It's not just one of the thirty-two. It's "American's Team," or whatever you want to call it. It's like New York, except it's in the middle of the country. The job opened up after the 2006 season when Bill Parcells retired as a coach for the third time in his career. The first two were after he had been with the New York Giants and New York Jets.

I spent a long time interviewing with Jerry Jones, the Cowboys' owner and general manager, and his son, Stephen, their executive vice president. It wasn't so much about Xs and Os, although both of them understand that part of it. It was more about how you run a football team, how you run practices, how you run training camp, how you teach players, how you handle discipline, and on and on.

A lot of what I've done as a coach comes from the seven rules of coaching that my dad followed:*

1. He would never have intrasquad scrimmages because he didn't want his players risking injury against each other. "What for? Houston's not on our schedule," he said.

2. He limited his drills to sixty-five to seventy-five minutes each day. As he explained: "I think a guy ought to have a certain amount of repetition, but he's gotta be convinced that he's gotta get better at repetition, not just do repetition for repetition's sake. Twelve repetitions in a two-minute period don't teach you as much as five repetitions with the thought, *I want to do something better this time.* If you want conditioning, wait 'til practice is over and run. The only thing I changed through the years on that is trying to convince the players to put in enough effort

running during practice so that they wouldn't need to do extra running after practice."

3. He always demanded extra effort. "If you don't like my attitude, see your friendly player rep," Daddy said.

4. He always wanted his players to show improvement every day. "If [a player] started out even with the guy he's competin' against and improves every day, well, three weeks from now he's better than the other guy and three months from now he's beatin' the hell out of him. A football season is like a football game; you try to be better in the fourth quarter. Most of the time, the team that progresses a little bit as the season goes is the better team."

5. He always invited players' families, including kids and dogs, to the Saturday practice before a Sunday home game, and would let them go home early together.

6. He expected his players to be self-motivated rather than driven by coaches. "You can't win today by embarrasin' football players," he said. "If I played for a guy who shouted at me, I'd sock him."

7. He never sought coaching advice from my mom. "I don't help her cook and she don't help me coach. She's a good wife that way. Oh, lemme tell you, she don't like to lose. She ain't friendly to me when we get beat but she's understandin'. She's gotta be. Hell, I've taken one week off in thirty-nine years. That don't exactly make me Husband of the Week."

Everything you can name, we covered in my interview with

the Joneses. The bottom line was that I had a lot of experience and was able to tell them how I did things with different teams. Jerry did ask what kind of defense I was going to play. I told him it was a 3–4, which Parcells had used, but I told him it was a different 3–4. Mine was more of a one-gap 3–4 than Parcells's two-gap style.

I knew Troy Aikman, the Cowboys' former quarterback, was pushing Norv Turner for the job. Turner had been Dallas's offensive coordinator. It made sense from the standpoint that offense was the strength of the team. The Cowboys had a good quarterback in Tony Romo and a good offensive line. They had a good running back in Marion Barber. They had good receivers, including Terrell Owens. But they had problems on defense. I went over with Jerry and Stephen where I had coached—that we had turned around the defense every place I'd been—even San Diego, which had the worst team in the league when I got there. I think that put it over the top for me.

I've had experience with all kinds of owners. Some of them are around the team all the time, some of them aren't. Some are kind of in between. I had a close relationship with Pat Bowlen, the Broncos' owner. He cried when he fired me. We hugged, and he cried. He told me he felt like if I had a better coaching staff, it would have helped me out. He said a lot of nice things, although he still fired me. Arthur Blank, the Falcons' owner, was good to me. He told me that the players had wanted me to stay on after he had made me the interim head coach, which he didn't have to say.

Jerry is really personable. I mean, you've got to like Jerry Jones. If you're around him, you've got to like him, unless you hate the Dallas Cowboys, which some people do. But as a person, he's likeable. He's fun to be around. His whole family is working with the team. They are a great family. I'm partial to family, myself.

You can like or not like what he does or doesn't do, but I thought it was a good situation. Just like in Buffalo, I was the vice president in charge of football, so I answered directly to the owner, which I thought was really good. I didn't have to go through an intermediary, which is usually the general manager. The general manager wasn't telling me what personnel I had. With Jerry, I was able to talk with the owner and the GM. I could say, "Hey, I like this guy," or, "I like that guy," or, "We can agree on this," or, "I don't like it, but that's who we're gonna keep."

Jerry Jones expects you to win the Super Bowl every year. He just puts a lot of pressure on his team to go to the Super Bowl and win it. He's won it three times before. He wants to win it again and again. And that's the other good thing about him. Some owners want to win, but they don't want to give the up-front bonus money to allow you to pick up the players to get it done. Jerry's willing to do that, so I thought he was a good owner in that sense.

If he had a Drew Brees, he was going to keep him, whereas San Diego let him go to get somebody else while Drew established himself as a Hall of Famer with the Saints. Jerry was willing to go out and get a guy like Terrell Owens, who also has Hall of Fame credentials. If you could convince him that a guy was going to help the team, he would pay the money to get him.

Terrell's personality rubbed people wrong. He was seen as being selfish, but I liked him because he worked hard and he played hard. I had been around selfish players before, but if they played hard, worked hard, that was a redeeming quality to me. Terrell had some great years in Dallas with us. He'd play hurt.

He didn't know how to say the right things at times. There were a lot of people against him, but I wasn't one of them.

At the start of training camp, Jerry said he expected to win the Super Bowl. He says it every year. He has certain ideas on things and you can go with it or tell him you don't like it, one or the other. He didn't mind you telling him you didn't like something either. He listened. Now once he makes up his mind on certain things, he's the boss. If he decided he was going to draft a certain player, he was going to take him, no matter what you or anyone else said.

When I joined the Cowboys, they already had an offensive coordinator, Jason Garrett. He had been the quarterbacks coach for the Miami Dolphins before they fired their entire coaching staff, which made him available. Once the season began, I liked what we had on both sides of the ball. We went 13–3, which was the best record in the NFL, and had a top-ten defense. We lost to the Giants in a home playoff game. We had the ball at the end of the game with a chance to win, but they stopped us. The Giants went on to win the Super Bowl, so you've got to think if we would have won that game, we might have won it all. You never know, because we had a really good year.

• • •

With Dad living in Goliad, which is about a five-hour drive from Dallas, I was able to see him more often. He could come out to see us, too. During one of his visits, he was shaking his head as he watched our prepractice warm-up drill where we had the first-, second-, and third-string offenses huddling before they would run a play and move downfield. He said, "You could

Spending a little quality time with Laurie in Dallas.

do it faster if you just run the right play from an audible, and not huddle every time." Which was true. Jason agreed, and that was how we ended up doing it from then on.

Although we were 13–3 that first season, Jerry wasn't happy because we didn't win it all. It's that simple with him. If you don't win it all, he's not happy. He was even less happy the second year when we went 9–7. Tony Romo was hurt for three of the games, and we lost two of them. We had a top-ten defense again.

We had another big year in 2009, finishing 11–5. We won the NFC East again, making it two out of three years that we won the division. We actually shut out Washington and Philadelphia back-to-back to end the regular season. The Eagles were averaging twenty-seven points a game. Then we beat them the following week in a wild card playoff game, 34–14, for the Cowboys' first postseason win in fourteen seasons.

The Minnesota Vikings beat us in the next round, 34–3, with Brett Favre at quarterback after he had gone from the

Green Bay Packers to the New York Jets. Our offense didn't have a good game at all. Minnesota was really good. The Vikings went on to lose to New Orleans in the NFC Championship Game. We had beaten the Saints during the regular season, so we felt good about our chances against them if we were able to get past Minnesota. To show you how strong the Saints were, the Vikings had thirty-one first downs to the Saints' fifteen and still lost. I thought they were the better team. The Saints ended up winning the Super Bowl against Indianapolis, but the Vikings were really good that year.

With one year left on my contract, I had my agent ask Jerry for an extension on my deal. It seemed like things were good, but they weren't. Or at least, they weren't good enough. The year before, when we went 9–7, the press wanted to fire me. Now here I was, with a 33–15 record and a playoff win in three seasons, and coming off an 11–5 year. I thought I'd get Jerry to extend my contract beyond the 2010 season. But he wouldn't.

Another factor was Jason Garrett had some head coaching opportunities. He got an offer from the Baltimore Ravens, and his agent evidently went back to Jerry and said, "If you give him what Baltimore is paying him as a head coach, he'll stay in Dallas as offensive coordinator." Jerry matched the offer and now Jason was making more than me.

I asked Jerry about it and he said, "Well, you know, we had to keep him."

"That just doesn't seem right to me," I said.

After our 9–7 season, when the offense struggled, Jerry said that maybe he should have let Jason take the Baltimore job rather than give him the big raise.

Jerry did agree to give me more money. He did it by adding an option year to the two remaining seasons on my contract.

It included a bonus that would only be paid if I finished the season as head coach.

"This is just for if you murdered somebody, or something like that, you wouldn't get the bonus," Jerry said. "And it's our option to pick up that extra year."

"Well, then that's not giving me another year if it's your option," I said.

I took the deal, although I still didn't think it was right. Jerry can do what he wants to do as owner, obviously. I just didn't think it was right that an assistant coach was making more than a head coach. He could have paid me more. He had plenty of money. Still does. But he's a businessman and his business side made that decision.

• • •

We began the 2010 season on a bad note with a 13–7 division loss to Washington. We didn't allow a touchdown on defense. We shouldn't have allowed the Redskins' defense to get one either, but right before the half, Jason asked me, "You want us to go for a score or just run the half out?"

"Yeah, okay," I said.

We ran a play and we got a ten-yard holding penalty. There were only four seconds left in the half. Jason called a pass. Tony Romo threw to our running back, Tashard Choice, who was four yards behind the line. DeAngelo Hall hit him; he fumbled; Hall picked up the ball and ran it in for a touchdown.

I didn't know Jason was going to run a play after having a ten-yard penalty and only four seconds on the clock instead of kneeling on the ball, which was what we should have done.

We lost to Chicago the following week before winning at Houston. Unfortunately, things just went downhill from there and we lost our next five games. Romo got hurt in the sixth game, against the Giants, so that just made things worse.

We hit rock bottom in our eighth game when we went to Green Bay and lost 45–7. It was one of those situations where if you get beat by a good team on the road and a lot of things go bad for you, the perception is you've lost the team as the head coach. Everybody's saying that. They think that.

For road games, I would fly out with the team but always fly back with Jerry on his private plane, mainly because he wanted to use that time for just the two of us to talk and to hear about what happened in the game from the coach's perspective. On the way back from Green Bay, I gave him my thoughts about the game, although I knew that he was hearing the same thing that was being said pretty much everywhere—that I had lost the team.

The next day, he called me into his office and said, "I'm going to make a change."

I asked him if I could stay on the job for one more game because I felt I would have a chance to go out on a winning note. We were playing the Giants on the road, and I said he could make the change after that game and start fresh with a new coach for our next game at home, which would be a week after the New York trip.

"No, no, I've made up my mind," Jerry said. "That's what I want to do."

Jason Garrett took over and the Cowboys won the next two games and ended up with five total victories to finish the year 6–10. I felt like—and I still feel like—we could have won those last two games as well. You never know when it's going to turn around, but that didn't happen.

One of the first texts I received after being fired was from Terrell Owens, who Jerry had decided to let go after the 2009 season. "I think you're a great coach, and I really appreciate what you did for me," Terrell said.

I hadn't had many players do that and I had been coaching for a long time. Players say nice things later on, or when they see me, but Terrell went out of his way to tell me that he thought I did a good job. At a time like that, when you've just been fired, it makes you feel a lot better.

I also felt good about my 34–22 record with the Cowboys. It's not tremendous, but it's still pretty good. That's still the tiniest of a fraction of a percent ahead of Tom Landry, the all-time winningest coach in the history of the franchise. People don't want to hear that, but it's a fact.

There really is no other head coaching job like the Dallas head coaching job—football fans in Texas are crazy about their teams. I was exposed to that being around my dad and the whole "Luv Ya Blue" era in Houston. We went 10–6, 10–6, and 11–5 with the Oilers, and still got fired. We were one of the winningest teams in the league for those three years, so that showed me that anything can happen. It all comes back to the fact that the guy who owns the team can do whatever he wants to do even if you don't think it makes a lot of sense.

As long as you work hard for him and do the best you can, that's all you can do. What I won't do is look back and say, "Well, I should have done this or I should have done that better." When it comes to owners, you just never know what's going to happen from one year—and sometimes one game—to the next.

CHAPTER EIGHT

"HEY, THEY CAN'T KILL YOU AND EAT YOU"

"There are people, maybe two or three, that ain't
gonna like you. Not everybody likes everybody.
My grandpa used to say, 'Just nod 'n grin.'"

—Bum Phillips
from *He Ain't No Bum*

My dad would always help me keep a little perspective during the tough times. I remember, in my last year as head coach in Denver, the fans were throwing things at me after one of our losses. They threw food and game programs, whatever else they could get their hands on.

It was right after Laurie's dad, Stinky, had passed away and we went down to Texas for the funeral. I came back during the same week, and after we got beat at home, the fans were vicious. They were just hollering, "Get rid of him!" Things like that. And then treating me like a human trash can. It reminded me of when that woman in New Orleans threw the beer on Daddy and basically drove him out of coaching.

I was really close with my father-in-law, so I was already pretty low. After that game in Denver, I was just dead. I just felt so bad. After that, I talked to my dad and told him what had happened and how I was feeling.

That's Wes holding my granddaughter, Ivy, who got to meet her great grandfather.

He said something that has stuck with me ever since: "Hey, they can't kill you and eat you."

I laughed at the time, but that might have been the best advice I ever got. It might be the best advice anyone in the whole coaching profession could get. You're always going to have to go through hard times. Even the most successful coaches in the league aren't immune. But it's important to remember that you can't let those hard times destroy you.

It's not cancer. It's not a life-threatening deal. It's not war. Psychologically, it can get to you, of course, but only if you let it. As long as you feel good about yourself and your family, as long as you feel good about how you do things, you can rise above everything else.

Sure, it tests you a little bit, because everybody's saying you're doing things wrong or you're not a good coach or you're stupid or whatever. But you go back and you say, "I'm doing it this way, I think this is what's best."

Coaching teaches you all kinds of life lessons. It teaches you how to deal with constant ups and downs, how to keep players and coaches on the same page when so many things are trying to pull them apart. It teaches you to understand that you're only as good as your last win, but that you can't spend too much time thinking about your last loss or it will tear you apart. It teaches you how to be stronger than you ever thought you were capable of being.

I didn't dwell on being fired then. I don't dwell on it now. I felt I did all I could do. Somebody else made that decision to fire me. Coaching is a different profession from others in the sense that, most of the time, somebody wants to fire you no matter what you do. Somebody's mad about what you're doing or not doing. If it's the guy that owns the team, then that's when you're in trouble. Bud Adams made the decision to fire us even after we won all those games with the Oilers. It's just a part of the profession.

"Hey, they can't kill you and eat you."

You've got to live with that. If you don't, then you shouldn't be in it. You shouldn't be in the NFL. You probably shouldn't be coaching high school football in Texas. They'll fire you in Texas if the mom of somebody on the school board doesn't like you. It can happen.

I still had a rooting interest in the Cowboys, though. My son, Wes, who got hired as a quality control coach my first year in Dallas, remained with the team. Wes first worked with the receivers, then I had him work with the quarterbacks, and then he started working with the offensive line.

I like to joke that Wes is the black sheep of the family because he coached offense. But he played quarterback in junior high, high school, and college. I played quarterback in high school, but I also played linebacker, and that's where I also played in college. I was really a linebacker playing quarterback. Wes was a pure quarterback. In fact, when he was in eighth grade in Denver, I went to one of his games that gave me the first sign that he might make a good coach one day. It was near the end of the game, his team was behind, and he kind of rolled out to throw a pass. The receiver was open going across the middle and Wes hesitated a little bit before throwing it to him for a touchdown.

After the game, I said, "Wes, why didn't you throw the ball when he was crossing the middle in the first place?"

"Well, there was a guy on the side there," he said. "If I would have thrown it sooner, he would have tackled him before he got to the end zone."

That's when I knew Wes had a good feel for football. He played quarterback at Texas El Paso, then spent one year as a student assistant coach there. He was young and still wanted to play, so he spent two seasons as a quarterback for the San Diego Riptide of the Arena Football League. When he finally got that out of his system, he was ready to go into coaching full time. He got his start as a quarterbacks coach at Division II West Texas A&M, and the team did really well. His quarterback, Dalton Bell, set school and Lone Star Conference records by throwing for 3,799 yards, thirty touchdowns, and thirteen interceptions.

Wes called me after their first intrasquad spring scrimmage, offense against defense. He was all excited.

"Dad, I got them," he said. "I knew they were going to blitz on the first play, so I ran the jail-break screen. We went eighty yards on the first play."

I treated Wes like my dad treated me. I said, "If coaching is all that you want to do, then that's what you ought to do. But if there's anything else you want to do, then you ought to do that and you shouldn't go into coaching." He made it clear to me that he wanted to coach.

Lee Hays, the West Texas A&M offensive line coach, became the offensive coordinator at Baylor and he took Wes with him to be his quarterbacks coach. Wes did a great job with the quarterback there as well. I got to watch him coach during spring training, and was impressed. When I was hired as head coach of the Cowboys, I hired him as a quality control coach.

What I should have done was give him a job as a position coach. He was good enough, or probably better, than some of the ones I had. But he was my son, so I didn't want anyone to think it was just nepotism, which was not the case whatsoever.

As an offensive quality control coach, he worked under Jason Garrett and was mainly responsible for analyzing video-tape of our offense. He would watch our previous four games and record which plays we ran out of certain formations, the personnel groups we used, and so forth. He would draw up all of the patterns the receivers ran and all the running plays, giving us complete picture of our tendencies to see how opponents were using them against us.

Wes also kept track of what each opposing defense did on each play—on first and ten, they played a twenty-seven defense; on second down, they went with a particular subpackage—whatever. He just analyzed everything and put it all together. He also put together PowerPoint slides for the position coaches to help them present whatever they needed to present to the players, and he helped out Jason with the game plan. Wes knew what he was doing. He was very meticulous about things, probably more detailed than I am.

When I left, he was assistant offensive line coach, working with Bill Callahan, but then they made him tight ends coach to replace John Garrett, Jason's brother, who also lost his job. I don't think it was Jason's decision to fire him. I think that came from Jerry Jones. But it worked out for Wes, because he was exposed to coaching every position on offense and that was a big part of what I wanted him to get out of working with me.

Having Wes on my staff, I got to see the father-son coaching relationship from the other side. I remember how much I enjoyed coaching with my dad. Now I got to feel that same joy of coaching with my son. Right before I hired Wes, he was coaching at Baylor. I thought, "Man, this guy's a really a good coach." Even though he's my son, I can recognize whether he's a good coach or not because I watched how he did the job. I could see he was great with people. I could see he worked really hard. I could see he was really smart.

It was like my dad used to say about me: "He knows what I know, but he also knows what he knows."

People want to accuse head coaches who hire their sons or brothers of nepotism. It's an easy thing to say, and maybe there are times when it's true. But the thing you always have to remember is that you can't fool the players when it comes to who you hire to coach them. You can't fake it, because the players know if someone can coach or not. They're counting on you to put them in the best position to succeed, and if they don't see that happening, they're not going to keep that to themselves. They don't mind telling anybody. They'll say it right to the guy's face, "Hey, you're hurting my profession, my chance for making a living."

It was just like when I first started with the Oilers as the defensive line coach. The players had no respect for the guy who had the job before me because he couldn't coach, and they ran all over him. I had to prove to guys like Elvin Bethea and Bubba Smith that I could coach. These are guys who've had a bunch of coaches before you, so they're going to know right away what you're all about.

The point isn't whether someone gets the job. It's whether they can do the job. As the head coach, you can find that out by seeing how they work with the players and how the players work with them.

Wes was upset the Cowboys fired me, but I told him, "Hey, this is part of coaching. You've got to go on. You love coaching. You've got to do what you've got to do. You could have been somewhere else, and your dad could have still been fired. It just so happened that we were on the same team. You've got a good job. You're married; you're starting a family. I think

you're gonna be a heck of a coach, and hopefully you're gonna be a third-generation head coach in the league, which would be pretty special."

I had no problems whatsoever with Wes remaining with the Cowboys. If you have a problem with something like that, then you shouldn't be in the business because you don't have that kind of control. You don't own the team. Those things can happen. And if it's good for him, which it was, I'm glad for him. I was glad that they kept Wes on the staff, because he's a good coach. He's a really good coach.

• • •

My relationship with my dad got better as we got older. It was great while I was coaching for him. I just loved those ten years together. That was a special time, being with him every day. But he was more of the generation where fathers didn't really tell their kids that they loved them. That changed as he got older. He would tell me how much he loved me, that he was proud of me, those kinds of things. I always felt the same about him, but I guess we told each other that more later on than we did earlier.

My dad enjoyed ranching. He thought it was the greatest thing ever when he got a tractor that had an air-conditioned cab with a CD player and stereo speakers. He was always playing Willie Nelson songs. We'd see him out there riding that tractor, plowing fields or whatever, even when it was dark. Sometimes we had to go out and tell him to come inside for dinner. He also had a bulldozer, and he'd go out and level the ground.

By this point, Dad and Mom had gotten divorced. It happened right after he left the Saints and I had gone on to the

Eagles. He called me in Philadelphia to tell me about it. It was difficult for me and the family overall. You just don't expect that to happen after forty years of marriage.

At sixty-five, he remarried. His second wife Debbie was a horse trainer. It fit what Daddy liked to do. They bought the ranch in Goliad. The sign at the entrance said BUM PHILLIPS, with a logo of a football with a cowboy hat on it. Debbie was good for him, because they could talk ranching; they could talk horses. She taught people how to ride cutting horses, which are used to herd cattle. They're sort of able to mimic a steer's movement, step for step, and get any of the strays back where they belong.

After I was fired from the Cowboys, Laurie and I got to spend some time with my dad and Debbie at the ranch. Each summer, we'd visit for a week or so. Now we were able to be out there during the season. It was very relaxing. He liked to sit there and watch the sun rise. He would say, "There's always something to do on a ranch. There's always something that needs fixing. Horses need to be fed, the cattle." It was a different life than what I'd been around, because I grew up in a football environment and lived my entire life like that.

At one time, Dad and Debbie had five hundred acres and a few hundred head of cattle. He called what he had there "rent-a-cows," because people paid him to put their cattle on his land and feed them. Then they'd take them to the lot, sell them for the owners, and he'd get a percentage.

Everybody was welcome in Daddy's house, even when he was coaching in Houston. He'd leave the door open, and if somebody knocked on the door, he'd say, "Come in." They'd say, "Hey Bum." He'd say, "Hey, there's beer in the refrigerator in there." He wouldn't even know who it was half the time.

Daddy liked to cook. He had never cooked before, but

Debbie got him to make pancakes, so he made pancakes for everybody in the morning. He started enjoying things like that.

He also liked to watch horse racing on TV. He always would pick the grey horse, if there was one in the race, because, being color-blind, that was the only one that looked different to him than the others. Anytime we went to the races, he had to bet on the grey horse.

One day, when I was a kid and color TVs were still new, Dad came home with one. He was all excited. He told my sisters and me, "Look what I got for everybody! A color TV!" We all started laughing. "Dad, you're color-blind, why?" We thought it was funny as heck, because he was proud he got that color TV.

Daddy and Debbie had the kind of house you'd expect, a

Maybe little Mac Phillips is going to be a fourth-generation football coach one day.

cowboy-looking place. He had a big collection of different spurs, the kind you wear on cowboy boots, on the mantle. There was a table where you could play dominos and an armoire loaded with pictures of the kids and grandkids.

There was a huge open area in the middle, which was where they had a big television. Daddy and I watched a lot of football together, which was great because we hadn't gotten to do that a lot. Dad sat in his recliner, I'd sit next to him on the couch, and over the course of five days we'd watch a bunch of college and NFL games. We got to second-guess coaches, which was kind of fun. Being with him helped get my mind off of everything that had happened.

The gals would come in and out, but it was mostly just my dad and me. Sometimes, we'd hear, "Hey, time to eat." If the game was good enough, we'd say, "Well, bring it over here. We'll watch the game and eat." Laurie or Debbie would have some sort of casserole or chicken, something simple. Dad would enjoy having a cold beer. I'd have my usual diet Dr. Pepper.

Those are the kind of father-son moments that you hold onto forever.

• • •

Right after the 2010 season, Gary Kubiak, who was the coach of the Houston Texans, fired his defensive coordinator, Frank Bush. Gary and Frank were good friends, but the Texans' defense ranked next to last in the NFL. He couldn't save his friend, no matter how friendly they were, so he contacted me shortly after he let Frank go.

I had a lot of history with Gary. When he was in high school, he was a ball boy for the Oilers during our training camp at San Angelo, Texas. Gary was a really good quarterback, and would eventually get a scholarship to play at Texas A&M and wind up as a backup to John Elway in Denver. When he was a ball boy, Gary would throw the ball with our quarterbacks and we would kid Gifford Nielsen, our backup to Dan Pastorini, "Hey, that ball boy over there can really throw the ball. You'd better watch out."

Gary actually saw some action in the 1991 AFC Championship Game that Denver lost in Buffalo when I was the Broncos' defensive coordinator. John got hurt late in the game, and Gary came in and was marching us down the field. He threw a pass to Steve Sewell, the running back, and he fumbled it on about the Bills' thirty-yard line to end the game.

When Gary told me he wanted me to interview for the Texans' defensive coordinator job, he said Bob McNair, the team's owner, was going to send his private jet to pick me up. When I'd interviewed for the same job with the Bills in 1995, they gave me a coach ticket and I had a seat in the back of the plane to Buffalo. So I'm thinking, *I've got a pretty good shot at this.*

My instincts were right. The Texans had a pretty good offense, but needed a lot of help on defense. Mr. McNair and Gary agreed that I could fix it. The job was mine if I wanted it. I wanted it.

The defense became the focus of the draft. We had the eleventh overall pick and we needed an outside linebacker to rush the passer in our 3–4 scheme. We liked Von Miller from Texas A&M, but he went second overall to Denver. We also liked Aldon Smith from Missouri. We thought he was the best pass rusher in the draft, but the San Francisco 49ers took him with the seventh choice.

Gary and Rick Smith, our general manager, started saying, "We're not going to be able to get an outside rusher, so we're going to go another direction, maybe offense, or whatever." When I heard that, I thought it was time to speak up.

"Wait a minute," I said. "I think we can put Mario Williams [who was an end] at outside 'backer, and take a defensive lineman. That would help us with the pass rusher, and also we'd get a defensive lineman to replace Mario."

They went for that idea. The next question was who that player would be. The best defensive lineman we figured would be there when we picked was J.J. Watt from Wisconsin. There was a whole group of us in that draft room—scouts, coaches, everybody—and Gary and Rick put it to a vote.

The show of hands was about fifty-fifty, but in my mind it wasn't close. Watt was the best player for us. I stood up and said, "I think we ought to take J.J. Watt. I think this guy can help us." I pointed out that even though he was a defensive lineman, he had more PBUs—passes broken up—than the defensive backs at Wisconsin. He would just swat balls down at the line of scrimmage. He had an incredible knack for doing that, along with the size (six foot five and 289 pounds) and athleticism.

"This guy's got a feel for football," I said. "He's rushing the passer, but he's also knocking the ball down, which is a great weapon on defense."

Bobby Grier, who was a longtime scout in the league working for the Texans, agreed with me. Even though Bobby and I stood up for J.J., it was Rick or Gary or Mr. McNair—or maybe a combination of those three—who would make the final decision. They decided to take him.

I always believed—and I got it from my dad—that when you're rushing the passer, you've got to be able to see the quarterback and make your moves while always knowing where he is. That's part of having a good feel for where you are on the pass rush.

Some guys get so locked into rushing the guy they're rushing against, trying so hard to beat him, they never know where the quarterback is. When I see a guy that's a pretty good pass rusher, but he also knows where the quarterback is at all times and can position himself to knock down the ball, that's a very special lineman. J.J. Watt was very special. He still is.

With J.J., we'd say, "We don't want you sitting at the line of scrimmage. We always want you moving."

As simple as that sounds, not everyone in this business agrees with that approach. Coaches are true to their own systems. They're all cookie cutters that way. They'll say, "We play this system, so everybody needs to play it this way. And if we don't have a guy that plays it this way, then we go get somebody else." Some coaches have been successful doing it like that, some haven't.

A lot of it's just ingrained in coaching. I came from a different school of thought, mainly because of my father. From when I first started, I thought if a guy can do some things, then you need to let him do them. If you've got a real tall, skinny guy and you've got a short, fat guy, the two of them can't play the same techniques because they aren't able to play them the same way. They don't have the same abilities. You're coaching individuals, and each is unique in his own way.

I have a system, but we change it according to the personnel. We'll fit it to the players that we have playing at that time. Then the next year, we'll still have the same basic kind of 3–4 look, but we'll do different things that fit the different players we have because your roster turns over every year.

• • •

I like to think I know a top-notch football player when I see one. My time in football has mostly been in coaching, but I've also had the chance to do some player-personnel evaluation. I started out that way because of my dad. For ten years, we went to different colleges and graded everybody. I didn't just look at the defensive guys. I graded offensive linemen. I graded tight ends. I graded running backs. I graded wide receivers. And as I said before, my dad always said I had a good eye for talent.

There are some places I've worked where they don't want your opinion at all. Or they want your opinion, but they don't value it. The personnel people run the personnel; coaches run the team on the field. But coaches are scouts. Some of them are better than others. Part of being a head coach is you have to realize who can evaluate personnel on your staff. If the offensive line coach is really good at picking offensive linemen, you weigh what he says. If he's terrible, you don't.

As soon as the season's over, coaches get ready for the draft as a staff. The scouts have been doing it all year. With a lot of general managers and scouts, coaches are just talking and nobody's really listening. They talk about the next guy and the next and the next, and that's it. The GMs and scouts say, "Thanks for your opinion," and move on.

But Dad took my opinion. He thought I was a good scout.

"I don't want to embarrass him," Daddy said, talking about me. "But he knows football players, and he stands by what he says. I like that. Don't make a mistake of not bein' decisive. If it's wrong, make the damn decision, or you'll end up bein' right in the middle on everythin'. If a guy's right in the middle, he don't have no beliefs at all."*

Besides Steve Largent, I found another Hall of Famer in Rickey Jackson, an outside linebacker in New Orleans, in the second round. When I went to Philadelphia, Buddy Ryan would only listen to the coaches. He wouldn't listen to the scouts.

In San Diego, we had the twelfth pick of the 2005 draft. Dallas had the pick right in front of us. We wanted an outside linebacker and DeMarcus Ware and Shawne Merriman were still available. A.J. Smith, our general manager, told me, "We're going to get one of those two."

"Yeah, that's great," I said. "Let's get one of them. Either one could be a really great player."

The Cowboys took Ware. We got Merriman. I got to coach both players.

In 1989, when I was coaching for Dan Reeves with the Broncos, we had the twentieth overall pick. We wanted a safety. Dan said there were two available with similar talent. One was Steve Atwater. I'm not going to identify the other one. But Dan said that besides being a really good player, Atwater also had great character. "We can't say that about the other player," Dan said. "Which one would you take?" I knew which one Dan wanted, and we took Atwater.

Steve had everything you wanted in a safety. He could cover. Play the run. Blitz. He also was a tremendous hitter.

Coaches have to rely on scouts to tell them what kind of person the college prospect is. They've gone to his trainers; they've gone to the coaches that they know to find out what problems the guy might have off the field. They find out about his work habits. My dad always wanted to know what kind of practice guy a player was, if he practiced hard or not, because that would tell him how much effort he put into preparing for each game.

Coaches enter the predraft process late, because they've been busy with their team all season. Hopefully, they're busy deep into the postseason, too. So as a coach, you're not going to find out all of that background information on your own. I basically can tell you whether a defensive lineman can rush the passer or not, because of his body movement, his foot movement, his feel for the pass rush, those kinds of things.

Level of competition is also part of it. You can get fooled a little bit on that because certain players look so good because their opponents just aren't very good. That's why I focus more on movement skills. You either have those or you don't, regardless of the competition.

We teach efficiency of motion. Can you change direction without taking too many steps? What kind of explosion do you have? It's about how you get your body from one place to another in a short area, a confined area—five, eight, ten yards—as opposed to the forty-yard dash. My dad used to say, "Hey, the difference in a guy who runs the forty in 4.8 and 4.5 seconds is this." He snapped his fingers twice. "All that really matters," Daddy said, "is which one can play football."

While we were recruiting at Oklahoma State, I told him about a kid that I thought would be a good player because he was a decathlete. My dad said, "Well, they don't give any points at halftime to the guy that wins the decathlon. We've got to have football players."

At the NFL Scouting Combine in Indianapolis, where about 250 college prospects are invited each year to work out for all of the teams, you get to have a fifteen-minute interview with each of sixty players of your choice. We had J.J. on our list. Bill Kollar, our defensive line coach, was part of the meeting.

"You don't hustle enough," Bill said.

J.J. hustles as much as anybody. I saw that on his college film. So J.J. kind of bowed up and said, "Hey, Coach, I think I hustle." What J.J. didn't realize was that Bill said that to all the defensive prospects just to see how they'd react. Some of them said, "Well, yeah, I could do better at that." J.J. gave it right back and I liked that about him.

At the end of J.J. Watt's rookie year, when he had five-and-a-half sacks and knocked down four passes, reporters asked me about how he played.

"He played great," I said. "A lot of people are saying he's a bust, but I think he's going to be a bust in the Hall of Fame." Nobody was really saying that, but I just thought it would be a good line to give to the media because J.J. played unbelievably the whole year. And his performance just went up from there.

He had great two-step explosion. That means even at a two-step distance from the ball, he can get to it in time to make a play. Great players can get from two yards quicker than other players can because they have that explosion or that quick twitch. Whatever you want to call it, J.J. had it.

We also found out he had a great feel for the game. He knew when he could and couldn't run around a block and make a tackle. And he could do the things it took to be a good pass rusher. Plus, he was a great worker.

• • •

These days it's harder to gauge what a college prospect is all about based on the interviews we conduct with them at the Scouting Combine, because their agents have them coached to say the right thing. That's especially true with the guys who have had a lot of trouble in the first place. They'll come in and say, "I made a mistake, I know you want to talk about it, I'm never going to do it again." Or, "I got caught smoking marijuana, it's the only time I've ever smoked it in my life." They can sound so convincing, so sincere, as if whatever happened was done by a whole different person.

You still can get a little feel for their personalities. There are a few of them that you can tell are kind of jerks. They just can't get away from that. But I would never go with a full evaluation on just an interview. You know that player's been interviewed by fifteen clubs and they all asked the same questions and he gave all of them the same answers.

We're in a cell phone society now, where after practice every guy has a cell phone in his hand. You worry about being close enough with the players, like my dad was, and guys getting to know each other because they're on the cell phone, texting or talking to somebody else. There's no real sense of bonding between teammates. It doesn't mean they aren't team guys. They just have a lot of other things taking away their attention. As a coach, you have to find a way to grab it and keep it for as long as you can.

Intelligence matters. I always say smart players get better. Finding them has gotten easier through the years. Almost all of the guys we get now are either close to graduation or have graduated. They'll go to summer school to finish their degrees. It used to be that a lot of guys we got hadn't finished school.

The other thing you look for with defensive players is the ability to react. Defense is reactive. You react to what you see, you react to how quickly you see things or how quickly you get off the football, when the ball is snapped, that kind of stuff.

We tried to build a teaching progression that could teach whatever level of player faster and better. That's part of what being a good coach is all about. If your material is easier to read or easier to comprehend, I think you get it across to the student better. And everybody—coaches and players—has to speak the same language all the time. This way, when I call the defense, I'm using the same words that the defensive line coach, linebackers coach, and secondary coach are using. We call whatever we're doing in a particular defense one thing so everybody understands it.

When I got to the Houston Texans, they were thirty-first in the NFL in defense and last in almost every other category. The league was negotiating a collective bargaining agreement with the players and when no deal was in sight, the owners locked the players out for that entire offseason. That meant we didn't get to work with them until the end of July, right before training camp. We still finished second in the NFL in defense because we had that great teaching progression.

The first thing I tell players is football is a simple game. All you have to do is know what to do, how to do it, and do it with great effort. The first thing we teach is alignment. Where do you line up for each play? Then we teach assignment. What are you supposed to do on that play? Then we teach technique. How do you execute that assignment?

We teach effort, too. Most players don't know what 100 percent full-out effort is all about. They think they're going full speed, but then they have to speed up to get to the ball. Well, they weren't going full speed if they have to speed up. A lot of times, players use their eyes. The ball's thrown, they turn and look for it, so they naturally slow down as they decide whether they can go get it or not. What we teach is, as soon as the ball is thrown, you keep running as you decide whether you can get to it or not.

We want players to finish every time, but your natural instinct is to slow down. Your natural instinct is not to go as hard as you can every play, especially if you don't think you can get to the ball. You have to overcome.

When I first got to the NFL as linebackers coach for the

Oilers, I watched the film from the year before to see who I would be coaching. I watched Robert Brazile, who was an outside linebacker, and I could see he played harder than anybody I'd ever seen. Every play was unbelievable. He would either make the tackle or he would be around the pile. If it was a forty-yard play, he was close to the play. I was watching film and I said, "This is unbelievable. I've never seen anybody play like this." And I marveled at it.

I went to Robert and I said, "I've never seen anybody play as hard as you play. How do you do that?"

He looked right at me and he said, "Coach, I practice that."

Sure enough, that was the way he practiced. We'd make the running backs run the ball like thirty yards down the field. Robert would run down there with one of them, and then he'd run back and be ready for the next play. We had a nine-on-seven drill—where you have nine offensive players working against seven defensive players—and every once in a while Robert would stand back there at free safety and just run to the ball.

I thought, *Just run to the ball, everybody can do that.* I mean, I did that as a college linebacker who never made it to the NFL. I knew if I didn't listen to that voice in my head that said, *Hey, I'm not going to get to the ball on time on this play,* or *The ball is way out there, I can't get to it,* I would be able to make the play. I felt I could teach players that, using Robert as an example. I'd say, "Look at what Robert does. You can do that, too."

When I got to New Orleans, Robert had been to the Pro Bowl six times, so all of our players with the Saints knew about him. I said, "You guys need to watch this guy play. You can play like that; you can play that hard; you can give that kind of effort." From then on, effort was something we always taught.

When I joined the Texans, we had a linebacker like that in Brian Cushing. He played a hundred miles an hour every play.

I told the other linebackers, "Hey, if everybody plays as hard as this guy, we're going to win." I had an example. Once you get a guy like that, the other guys try to play the same way.

We made the playoffs our first two seasons, going 10–6 in 2011 and 12–4 in 2012. Both times we lost in the divisional round. In 2013, the defense finished seventh in the NFL, but we went 2–14. Our quarterback, Matt Schaub, went five straight games where he threw an interception returned for a touchdown. We replaced him with Case Keenum, and he fumbled in the end zone for a touchdown the next game.

As we were heading off the field at halftime during a game against Indianapolis, our head coach, Gary Kubiak, fell to the ground. I just saw him out of the corner of my eye and assumed he had tripped or something, so I just kept jogging in with the rest of the team. All of a sudden, Rick Smith came in and told me, "Gary's gone to the hospital and we need you to take over the second half."

I was kind of shocked, just like everyone else. At first, there were reports he had a heart attack, but then later it was determined he had some sort of temporary blockage in a blood vessel in his brain.

When we came out for the second half, we had to tell the officials that I was now acting as the head coach. I was in charge of calling timeouts and other game-management stuff. Other than that, I just called the defense, as usual, while Rick Dennison, our offensive coordinator, called the offense. I didn't do a very good job as head coach, because we blew a 21–3 half-time lead and lost 27–24.

With three weeks left in the season, Gary was fired and I was offered the interim head coaching job. I said I would only take it if they would interview me to be the full-time head coach after the season. They agreed. Having been through it twice before, I knew my chances of winning were slim to none—especially when you've got a team that was on an eleven-game losing streak.

In the second-to-last game of the season, the Broncos came to Houston. They had a big lead late in the game, but their coach, John Fox, still was throwing bombs because he was trying to get Peyton Manning a passing record. The final score was 37–13.

I went up to Fox after the game. I told him he was a real chickenshit and that I didn't appreciate him running up the score.

He said, "Well, we didn't. Peyton just needed to get that record."

I said, "Well, you don't need to do that to anybody. I just don't think that was right."

A year earlier, we had beaten the Broncos in Denver, but we didn't run up the score. You don't try to embarrass the other team just to break some record.

We ended the season with a loss at Tennessee. The Texans interviewed me, but it was just a token deal. Once again, I was looking for work.

As Daddy always said, "There are two kinds of coaches in this business. Them that get fired and them that's gonna get fired."

CHAPTER NINE

FROM UNEMPLOYMENT TO THE SUPER BOWL

"We got here by bein' a lot of little people, not
by bein' big people. In this game, the minute
you lose, everythin' goes out the window.
So don't let it go to your head."

—Bum Phillips
from *He Ain't No Bum*

I COULDN'T BELIEVE THAT I WAS GOING TO SPEND AN ENTIRE offseason without working for an NFL team, but that was what happened in 2014 after the Texans fired me. I'm not sure what was keeping me from being hired, although my age of sixty-seven probably didn't help. I also had a year left on my contract at a pretty big salary. Late in my second season with the Texans, Tampa Bay wanted to talk to me about its head coaching job when we were in the playoffs. Bob McNair, our team owner, said to me, "You know, I'd rather you not do that, because of the playoffs and so forth." So I didn't talk with the Buccaneers.

It probably would have been my last shot at getting a head coaching job. However, Mr. McNair did come back and give me a new deal that made me the highest-paid assistant in the league. It was nice of him to do that. It was a reward for turning around a defense that went from thirtieth in the NFL to second in our first year and then ranked seventh in each of the next two seasons. But when other teams heard about my salary after I got fired, they said, "You know, we can't pay you what you were making in Houston."

After the 2014 season, a few assistant coaches had called to say if they got a head coaching job, they'd like to have me as their defensive coordinator. Tony Sparano had been the interim head coach in Oakland and thought the Raiders would hire him. Pat Shurmur, who had been the offensive coordinator in Philadelphia after two years as head coach in Cleveland, had another shot at a head coaching position. Frank Reich, who was the offensive coordinator in San Diego, also called me. He thought he had a chance with the Jets or Buffalo. All three of those guys had interviews, but none of them were hired.

I felt my record spoke for itself. I had consistently coached very good defensive teams. Beginning in 2005 with the Bills, I went to the playoffs in my first year with six teams in a row. I

thought real football people around the league would recognize those accomplishments. I thought everything was going to be okay. It wasn't. The 2015 offseason began and I was still out of work.

Finally, I got a call to interview with the Washington Redskins. Jay Gruden, their head coach, had fired his defensive coordinator, Jim Haslett, and wanted to talk with me about the job. By this point my son Wes was the Redskins' tight ends coach, so I was looking forward to the possibility of us working together again. But my interview with Jay was strange, to say the least. I'd had unusual interviews before—like the one with Marty Schottenheimer that took forever because he asked a million questions about the 3–4 defense—but I had never gone through something quite like this.

When Jay was the offensive coordinator in Cincinnati and I was with the Texans, I faced the Bengals twice in the playoffs, after the 2011 and 2012 seasons, and beat them both times—31–10 and 19–13. I felt he knew my credentials and might have been impressed with the things we were able to do in the previous three games in which we had beaten the Bengals, including one game during the regular season.

We watched a lot of tape of the Texans' games versus his offense. It seemed to me a lot of the plays were of when Cincinnati did well. Most of the interview was about that. I thought we should have talked more about philosophy, technique, concepts, and my record, but he was the one interviewing me.

After the interview I told Wes of my disappointment. I felt Jay didn't have as much regard for my coaching as I'd hoped he would. He ended up hiring Joe Barry, a friend of his, to be defensive coordinator. Joe had been with the Chargers, whose defensive coordinator was John Pagano. John had been my linebackers coach when I was the defensive coordinator in San Diego, so Joe basically learned my defensive system through John.

Although I didn't get the job, I was happy for Joe because I think he's a good, young coach. Of course, the main reason I had even considered going to Washington was for the chance to work with my son again. But I know Wes has enjoyed working with Jay, and they've done a good job with the Redskins.

Meanwhile, the Broncos hired Gary Kubiak to replace John Fox as their head coach. They were trying to get Vance Joseph to be their defensive coordinator. He was the secondary coach for the Bengals and he'd had the same job when I was with the Texans. But Mike Brown, the Bengals' owner, wouldn't let Vance out of his contract. (After spending the 2016 season as defensive coordinator for the Dolphins, Vance would become the Broncos' head coach in 2017 as the replacement for Gary, who decided to retire.) After that, the Broncos called me, so I was obviously the second choice.

I was disappointed that they thought somebody else would do a better job, especially because I had been with Kub in Houston, but that was the way it was. It's just like when somebody takes your place after you're fired, or you take somebody else's place and you get the job. You do the best you can and you don't worry about how you got the job. You just make the most of the opportunity. It didn't make me more determined to succeed. It didn't make me want to try harder—if you're not already doing the best you can, you shouldn't be in it. If you don't love it enough to deal with the fact that you're always in danger of being fired or that you're going to be passed over for jobs, you shouldn't be in it.

• • •

Denver was a good situation for me in that Bill Kollar and Reggie Herring, two guys with whom I had worked with the Texans, were already on the staff as the defensive line and inside linebacker coaches. Most of the time, I have to teach the coaches how I want things done and what the procedure is. After that, you want to let people coach. You don't want to take too much away from them, especially when they're good coaches who know how to teach the defense.

After getting blown out by the Seattle Seahawks 43–8 in Super Bowl XLVIII, the Broncos made a point of getting stronger on defense. They picked up several defensive players in free agency: outside linebacker DeMarcus Ware, cornerback Aqib Talib and safety T. J. Ward. The next season, they were third in overall defense, which was good. But I knew I could make the defense even better by switching from the 4–3 to my 3–4 defense.

The first thing I did after taking the job was what I always do: I figured out what our strengths and weaknesses were. We had to see who our pass rushers were, who our cover guys were, who our man-to-man corners were. We ended up having three good corners—Bradley Roby, Chris Harris, and Aqib Talib—so we played a lot of three-corner defense throughout the year. About 20 percent of the time, we played with Roby, Harris, and Talib.

If you've got good enough players, you need to get them in the game. If they're good enough to play and help you, then you've got to find a place for them. If you have corners that can cover, you put them all in the game at once. If we've got a bunch of guys that can rush the passer, you do the same thing.

Before I got there, they had a good defensive end in Malik Jackson, but they didn't play him very much. They had a really good outside linebacker in Von Miller, who wasn't rushing all the time yet had the skills to be a great pass rusher. He was playing Sam linebacker, which put him on the strong side, across from the tight end and the opponent's biggest tackle on all of the run plays. It also had him involved in a lot of pass coverage. We wanted to get Von more involved in rushing the passer, so we moved him to Will, on the weak side.

The players knew about me, and because of my track record, they trusted that they would be in good hands with me running the defense. Remember, the players are looking for something too. As a player, any time you don't do well, or don't do what you think you can, you want whatever it takes to become better. The fact that my reputation preceded me made my job a lot easier. It also helped having a guy like DeMarcus Ware, who had played for me in Dallas.

Everything was different from my last time with the Broncos in 1994. Even Pat Bowlen, the owner, was different. He was suffering from Alzheimer's. One of the first days I was there, he was in the dining hall for lunch, and Fred Fleming, who had been with him a long time, said, "Wade, just go over and say hello to him."

"How's he doing?" I said.

"Well, not good, but just go say hello to him."

I walked over to Pat, stuck out my hand and said, "Hey, Pat, Wade Phillips." He gave me a blank stare. He just said, "Pat Bowlen." I'd worked for him for six years. I was his head coach for two years. He cried when he fired me. And he didn't remember me.

Pat was such a vibrant guy, a strong personality, and fun to be around. That was a sad moment.

• • •

I had the great fortune of being with two of the best quarterbacks in NFL history during both of my coaching stints in Denver. One was John Elway, who was now our general manager. The other was Peyton Manning, our quarterback when I got there in 2015. He wasn't the same guy physically even from two years earlier, when I had last gone against him while in Houston, but he still could do things from a mental standpoint that set him apart.

Everybody says you have to have a great quarterback to win. That was especially true with Peyton. We beat him early in his career, because it was his first year in the league. While I was with the Chargers, we really had a great game against him in San Diego. We sacked him a whole bunch of times. The next time I faced him, in Indianapolis, was a different story. With us leading in the fourth quarter, the Colts had a fourth down and eight or ten on their own thirty-yard line. If they punted, I think the game would have been over. Manning went to the sideline and talked the coaches into going for it. They ended up getting the first down, scoring, and beating us.

Those kinds of things make you realize what a great quarterback can do. I played against him plenty of times, and he was hard to beat. The problem with playing against him was that he was the best at recognizing a weakness in your run defense and calling a run at the line of scrimmage to a specific spot to take advantage of it. He not only audibled to passes, which a lot of quarterbacks do, but he audibled to running plays.

Peyton could throw you off balance with the running game, and he did it a lot. His teams scored a bunch of touchdowns in the red zone running the ball because he'd spread the defense out with the formation, and when he saw the defense didn't have enough people in the middle to stop the run, he'd audible to a handoff and they'd score.

That's different than most quarterbacks, and that's because Peyton knew what the opposing team was doing. Any time you gave any kind of indication that you were going to blitz him one way or the other, he would change the protection and give himself enough time to throw the ball.

He worked tremendously hard with the receivers all the time to get on the same page with them, so they'd know where the ball was coming and when. Tom Brady does the same thing. You look at who's leading the league in receptions and it's some guy you never heard of, and he's probably playing for the Patriots.

The great ones throw the ball better than most other quarterbacks. They throw the ball with precision, on time. It doesn't matter who their receivers are. One season, the Steelers were without their Hall of Fame receivers, Lynn Swann and John Stallworth, for the first six or eight games, and the two backup receivers were the leading receivers in the league. That's because Terry Bradshaw was the quarterback.

The great ones also know how to protect themselves by anticipating how you're going to pressure them. Peyton knew if it was going to be a four-man rush, if it was going to be a six-man rush, if it was going to be a blitz. He'd check out where a guy was standing on defense and know if that guy was going to blitz, like if a safety was seven yards off the line instead of ten. Most other quarterbacks never even notice, but Peyton did a lot more intensive studying than most other quarterbacks. That was why we made our defensive players look at themselves and answer this question: *Are you giving anything away?*

We would try to counter what Peyton did at the line with what we called a "Hollywood." That was our way of letting our guys know we wanted them to act like they were going to come on a blitz, but not actually do so. Peyton would recognize those things, so we would tell our players to wait until there were ten seconds left on the play clock before we gave away our true alignment. At under ten seconds, you figure it's too late for him to change the original play he called.

If you started doing it earlier, and he picked it up, he was going to find a weakness in your pass coverage because there's a weakness in every coverage. Man-to-man, zones, whatever it is, there are weaknesses. He could recognize what coverage you were in and then he'd audible to a play that would go right for that weakness.

If both of your safeties were back ten yards and all of a sudden one of them came creeping up straight towards the tight end, he knew you were man-to-man. Then he audibled to a crossing route. Your corners come up and show two-deep zone, where both of your safeties line up deep, and he'd audible to a two-deep zone route.

If he saw a weakness in the run defense, he'd audible to a running play. That was why you wanted to make him run the play that he originally called, if you could. He still could beat you with that. Of course, defensive players will get impatient and want to show what we were doing at fifteen seconds. That's why, when we practice, we have the defense look at the play clock as well as the offense.

I don't know if anybody has been better than Peyton at beating everything. Let's put it this way. The roll call for guys who can do that doesn't take very long. He had it all, including a short passing game that was just phenomenal. Peyton was tremendous at throwing those quick slant routes. He was just so accurate. He knew where to go with the ball, but he also had his favorite pass plays that he could go to, and he could find his receiver no matter what defense you were playing. Even if guys were double covered, he still would complete passes to those guys, because he had such a good arm and great precision.

• • •

We won the AFC West with a 12–4 record. That meant we had to win two playoff games at home to get to Super Bowl 50. The first one was against the Steelers, who had beaten us 34–27 during the regular season. We had control of the game through the first half, then had a terrible second half. Brock Osweiler, who was starting at quarterback for an injured Peyton Manning, was bad through the final two quarters and we were terrible on defense.

In spite of that, we beat the Steelers 23–16 in the divisional round of the playoffs. Their last points came on a field goal they kicked with twenty-four seconds left to set up an onside kick that we recovered to seal the win. The key was that we stopped their running game and made them one-dimensional. Up to that point, Ben Roethlisberger, Pittsburgh's quarterback, had averaged more than thirty points a game.

After that, we played the New England Patriots in the AFC Championship Game. We had played the Patriots in the regular season, too, and beat them in overtime 30–24. They got the ball at the end of regulation, and kicked a long field goal to tie the game. The Patriots won the coin toss and Tom Brady was cheering, figuring they were going to go right down and score a touchdown to win the game. I just thought, *Man, that is kind of arrogant. Hey, you think you're gonna score on us?* But we sacked him, forced them to punt, got the ball back, and C. J. Anderson ran forty-eight yards for a touchdown to give us to win.

Of course, Brady is as good as I've gone against at quarterback. He's a competitor. My thinking he was arrogant was about his competitiveness, not anything against him. He had beaten us before, just like Manning did when I was at Houston and the

Broncos threw that touchdown pass they didn't need to throw, and Manning was excited about setting a record at our expense. Whenever Brady or Manning scored a touchdown against us, they would do that fist pump. I certainly don't like that, because you don't get to do that to them.

When we faced the Patriots in the AFC Championship Game, we felt we could stop their running game, just as we had the Steelers'. And we did. That forced them into passing situations, which was something they could do well, like the Steelers, but defending the pass and rushing the passer are also strengths of ours.

We had different strategies against each of them, because of the way they threw the ball and who they threw the ball to. Roethlisberger threw it to everybody except the tight end, Heath Miller. We knew we could match up against the tight end really well, so we concentrated more on their wide receivers and taking away the longer passing game than the shorter one. With New England, it was more about defending the shorter passing game.

The Patriots had beaten the Chiefs 27–20, with Brady completing twenty-eight of forty-two passes for 302 yards and two touchdowns. Watching film, most of those passes were for 5 yards or less, and they turned them into longer plays. That's what the Patriots do. We weren't worried about being able to stop the short passing game, but it's a two-edged sword because when you focus on stopping the short throws by playing more shallow coverage, they're going to throw it deep.

But we had enough of a pass rush that it was harder for them to throw it deep. That was when Brady got hit and got sacked. We sacked him four times and hit him seventeen times. Not only was it the most he had ever taken, but it also was the most hits on a quarterback in the playoffs in fifteen years.

We knew they weren't going to run it, and they couldn't run it, because we were basically rushing the passer and playing the run off of that. They were trying to spread out our defense by using three or four receivers, because Brady can pick you apart that way. But when you spread everybody out, it puts all of the pressure on your offensive tackles. They're not getting any help from a tight end or a running back making a chip block, and our guys are winning their one-on-one matchups with those tackles.

Being hit that much would bother any quarterback, and Tom Brady was no exception. No quarterback wants to get hit once, let alone seventeen times. Part of playing good pass defense is hitting the quarterback, or making him throw the ball faster than he wants to, or covering receivers. Pass defense was our strength. Passing was their strength. It was just strength on strength.

We fooled Tom with our coverage, which is saying something because he isn't fooled very often. He thought we were playing one-on-one coverage, but we had a safety out there and that helped us intercept him twice. Then with 1:34 left on the clock and with us holding a 20–12 lead, we basically had them beat. It was fourth and ten from the fifty-yard line. A stop there and it's game over.

Brady hit his great tight end, Rob Gronkowski, for a forty-yard gain to the ten-yard line. By that point, our starting safeties—Darian Stewart and T. J. Ward—had left the game with injuries, so we were really shuffling back there. It was hard to make the calls that we wanted to call, because we didn't have guys in there that had played them. We were doubling Gronkowski, and they still hit the big play on the fourth down.

We were able to force them into another fourth-down situation from our four-yard line with seventeen seconds on the clock. They would have to score a touchdown and get a two-point conversion to tie the game. Once again, Brady threw to Gronkowski. We doubled him that time, too, although this time we had one of our cornerbacks, Chris Harris, as part of the coverage. Gronkowski just swatted him out of the way, because he has the size and strength to do that, and caught the ball.

He's one of the best tight ends of all time. When I was with the Oilers, we faced Dave Casper, the Raiders Hall of Famer who was a tremendous blocker and receiver. We also had a Hall of Fame tight end in Shannon Sharpe during my first stint with Denver. Gronkowski is certainly in that group.

Now, the Patriots were going for two points to get the tie and force the game into overtime. We had worked a lot on defending against two-point plays during the year, and it paid off. We'd stopped the Bears earlier that year on a two-point attempt on the last play of the game to prevent them from tying us. We used a similar two-point defense against the Patriots.

It started with our pass rush. DeMarcus Ware was in the backfield so fast, Brady had to start running to his right, which threw off the whole play for New England. He then tried to throw it to one of his most reliable receivers, Julian Edelman, who was being covered by Aqib Talib. Talib tipped the ball, and Bradley Roby intercepted.

There were still twelve seconds left, which was enough time for the Patriots to try to recover an onside kick. I'm always nervous, and I was nervous then. But I never lost control. I just don't think that players can depend on a guy who loses it, especially in those critical situations. I'm always trying to think of what's going to happen on the next play, what we need to do the next time they get the ball. You've got to be in control. If you're emotional and lose your mind and lose your senses, you're not helping anything. You've got to be thinking clearly.

Kub came over to me and said, "They've got twelve seconds

left. They're gonna try to set up a sixty-yard field goal. You've got to have a defense to stop them."

"Coach, I'll be ready," I said. "If they get the ball, I'll have a call ready." They never got the ball. Shiloh Keo recovered the onside kick for us. Game over. We were going to the Super Bowl.

I walked over to Bill Belichick, shook his hand, and said, "Y'all have got a great team and had a great year."

He just said, "Go win the next one."

The first thought that crossed my mind after that game was that I had gone from unemployment to the Super Bowl—the second one of my coaching career. I wrote that in a tweet right after the game and I got over a million retweets, so people recognized it. That was a pretty neat deal.

I just thought it was fantastic. It wasn't a feeling of vindication or anything like that, because I knew that winning the conference championship wasn't going to be enough. I had been to the Super Bowl and lost before, in my first stint with Denver as a defensive coordinator. But I was excited about having this second opportunity, mainly because I hadn't had a job the year before.

· · ·

The game is always evolving, and when you've been in it as long as I have, you have to keep up with those constant changes. It was a lot simpler when I first started, but offenses have gotten more complicated and that means the defenses have to become more complicated.

When I first started, everybody ran a two-back offense on first, second, and third down. Then came the first big change when the Dolphins started putting a receiver, Nat Moore, at running back on third down. They wanted to match him up against your linebacker, knowing the linebacker would be too big and too slow to cover a receiver out of the backfield. All of a sudden we had to come up with different personnel groupings, replacing linebackers with defensive backs on third down.

After that came what we call subpackages. You had your base defense, a 3–4 or 4–3, but you also had to be ready to substitute players so you had the right people on the field when the offense went with something different, such as eleven personnel (one back and one tight end). From there you had teams, like the Oilers when they had Hall of Fame quarterback Warren Moon, using ten personnel (one back with no tight ends), for an offense they called the "run and shoot." It was just constant passing, to the point where even if they were leading late in the game, they kept on throwing because they didn't use a tight end to block for the run.

Today, different teams use different personnel groupings to do whatever they want to do: thirteen personnel (one back, three tight ends) to run more, twelve personnel (one back, two tight ends) to be a more multiple offense with the ability to run or throw, and twenty-one personnel (two backs, one tight end) to be more of a hammering type offense on play action. They've also gone to empty (no backs, no tight ends, and five receivers) a lot more.

Then there's the NFL's latest offensive trend, which is the zone read. It's what all of the colleges are running and you have to have a quarterback who can run well, because after he takes the snap, he either fakes the handoff and runs himself or gives it to the running back. If he sees that nobody is picking him up, he's going keep it and run. If he sees the defense doesn't have eight defenders bunched near the line to stop the run, he's going to hand off.

You've also got the quick passes, the jail-break screens, where the throw is made behind the line of scrimmage and the receiver has a wall of blockers set up in front of him to one side or the other. Now the one good thing from a defensive perspective—and I've been fighting to keep it this way—is that the NFL doesn't have the college rule where, if the catch is made behind the line of scrimmage, the blockers can go down the field.

That's what kills defenses, especially if you're blitzing. It doesn't take much for a quarterback to throw the pass, because he's only throwing it five yards and sideways. But when you get those linemen downfield and you have blitzers coming forward, once the receiver catches it, he's got a whole wall of people in front of him. It's like a punt return. The NFL rule is that the offensive linemen can't cross the line of scrimmage until the guy catches the ball. But they're stretching that a lot and officials are letting offenses get away with it. To me, that's hurting defenses and hurting football.

If it starts becoming like what you see with colleges, you're going to get a lot of 45–44 games like they're having at the collegiate level. They're just completely taking away what the defense can do. If you say it's alright for linemen to already be down the field when the screens are thrown and to run pick plays, where receivers get in the way of defensive players to allow other receivers to get open, those two things would kill defenses. In many cases, they already have.

But even as defenses have become more complicated, it's important that you don't make what you're doing too difficult to learn because you don't have much time to make it work. With our defense, the one constant is that we've always tried to teach it in a way that means players can grasp it quickly and not make many mistakes the first time they play in it. That's what's helped us all along. You constantly tweak things, but it always comes back to the fact that defense is pretty simple. It's "know what to do, how to do it, and do it with 100 percent effort."

As Daddy said, "Sometimes we get coaching so hard that we overcoach. Football's an automatic-reflex game. It's a game that if you do it well, you don't have to think about it. Where you get into trouble is a guy havin' to think. That's why rookies have a hard time makin' it. They don't have enough time to get their habits so doggone ingrained in them. They get so tied up with the technique they're tryin' to teach 'em that they don't get into the block. Then it looks like, 'Boy, he's not tryin'.' He's tryin' but he's thinkin'.

"You can overcoach a guy a helluva lot easier than you can undercoach him. I've seen more players overcoached than undercoached. The name of the game is tackle the guy with the ball. All that other stuff, like how you get there to tackle him, is immaterial as long as you get it done."*

We go out of our way to try to make it sound simple to the players, which is part of our teaching philosophy. Some coaches will say, "Hey, this defense is so complicated, it's going to take you a couple of years to learn it." We take the opposite approach. We say, "This is a simple defense. You're going to know where to line up, you're going to know what your assignment is, and then we're going to teach you techniques to play that assignment. And we're going to play harder than everyone else plays."

This is what I handed out to our defensive players in our first meeting in Denver:

PHILOSOPHY OF THE
DENVER BRONCOS' DEFENSE

Our basic defense is an attacking style. The Broncos' philosophy on first and second down is to stop the run and play outstanding pass defense. We will play zone, man to man, and blitz in any situation. On any down we may utilize different fronts or different personnel groups.

In all situations, we will defend the inside or the middle of the field first—defend inside out. Against the run, the Broncos will not allow the ball to be run inside. We want to force the ball outside. Against the pass, the Broncos will not allow the ball to be thrown deep down the middle or inside. We want to force the ball to be thrown short and/or outside.

The trademark of the Denver Broncos' defense is aggressiveness and physical play. We will be physically strong at the line of scrimmage and will hustle and pursue relentlessly. We will be hard and sure tacklers. The Denver Broncos will be successful on defense because we give 100 percent physical effort and do not make mental mistakes. To eliminate mental errors, we must fully understand the concept of the defense and be disciplined to play the defense called. We will not allow big plays against us.

The Broncos defense must perform efficiently inside our twelve yard line (red area) and on the goal line. We cannot allow our opponents to run the ball into the end zone. We will have a great run defense with tight pass coverage. We will prevent touchdowns and force field goal attempts by playing outstanding team defense.

Defensively, we must adapt to every situation

that presents itself and execute successfully. This requires good communication, teamwork, and personnel substitution. Some defensive situations that occur are: second and long, third down, fourth down, two minute, no huddle, short yardage, red area, goal line, two-point play, four minute, protecting a lead, opponent backed up, and no huddle. We will prepare for and handle all situations.

Finally, our job is to take the ball away from the opponents' offense and score or set up good field position for the Broncos' offense. We must knock the ball loose, force mistakes and cause turnovers. Turnovers win games! We will be alert and aggressive and take advantage of every opportunity to come up with the ball.

** DEFENSE WINS CHAMPIONSHIPS **

We talked about being number one in the league in defense, and we were for all but two weeks of the season. And then we wanted to be the best pass defense, which we were. And we wanted to have the most sacks, which we did. Even in the running game, we gave up the lowest average per carry in the league. We were number one in basically every category.

You also have to make an effort to get to know your players, something I did in Denver and everywhere else I've worked. You can't be aloof with them. When I speak at coaching clinics, I always say, "Go talk to your players before and after practice. Take some time with them so they get to know you as well as you get to know them."

There's always an age gap between coaches and players to

start with. It only gets wider if the only time they see you is on the field, when you're chewing them out. Then you're back in the office watching film, while they're dressing to go home. There's no relationship that way. It's more like you're a dictator. If they know you, and they know your intentions are good and that what you're doing is trying to help them be better players, be a better team, I think it just works out better.

We had a lot of strong personalities on our defense in Denver, just as we did with the Oilers way back in the 1970s. One of the strongest was Aqib Talib. He was like Richard Pryor. He was hilarious. He was a little irreverent at times. Not everybody was going to like it, but a lot of what he said was really funny. Usually he was exaggerating about something. He was loud. It was not all in fun, though. Once we got into the playoffs, he ripped into a few guys for being late to a meeting. I thought, *Wow! This is the way it ought to be, with players holding each other accountable.*

You don't always coach the defense as a group. You have to do individual coaching as well and know when the right time is to take a player aside and have a conversation. There are some guys you can walk up to and put your arm around them to make a point. With other guys, you've got to holler to get through to them. Most of the time, if you tell players the reasons that you have them doing certain things, they'll respond well. It doesn't always have to be something related to a specific thing they're doing football-wise. Sometimes, you just want them to know, "Hey, this is fun."

Part of the connection I made with the defensive players on the Broncos was through music. They'd be playing rap music and some of them started dancing to it, so I'd do a little bit of dancing myself, sort of copying what they were doing, and they laughed. They were doing the stanky leg, and I tried to emulate them or just tried to mess around with them. They'd say, "Coach is with it." A big song they liked was the one by Drake, "Started From the Bottom." When I started singing it and they realized I knew the words, they said, "Wow! He actually listened to some of our music."

As with pretty much every NFL and college team nowadays, we played rap and different kinds of popular music during practice. Sometimes the person in charge of playing it would throw in something by the Four Tops or a classic rock song by AC/DC. It helped make the players looser. It seemed to rev up the practice a little bit because it got people going. We turned it off at certain points, because we were coaching and we wanted the players to hear what we said.

But I have some rap songs on my iPod. I have country music and oldies, too, but I mix a little rap in there. To me, it's just like any music. Some of it I like and some of it I don't like. I don't like all the curse words, but I understand that's a part of what the music is all about.

As I witnessed from being around my father, I think you can be friends with your players and still be successful as a coach. Some people think coaching is just hollering at them at practice and then going in and watching film, and then coming back out and hollering at them again in the meeting. But it's okay to do other things like sing and dance around with them. I'm not doing it just because I think it's going to get me in good with the players. I do it because I like to be around them, for one thing.

I also think they respect what I'm doing and they respect me as a person. It's not like we're going to go out together that night or anything like that. But it helps them get to know you and it helps you get to know them. I think you learn better and you play better when you like the people who are coaching you and are comfortable around your coaches and believe in them.

CHAPTER TEN

"THE MISTAKES
ARE MINE"

"If I could be remembered for one thing, that
would be for bein' myself. You may not always be
right but do what you think is right; and if you're
wrong, have the ability to admit you're wrong.
Both are damn important. Maybe you ain't got
the market cornered on brains, but it's human
nature to always want to be right."

—Bum Phillips
from *He Ain't No Bum*

MEDIA NIGHT IS WHEN THE CIRCUS PART OF THE SUPER BOWL officially begins. Players and coaches from each team take turns being interviewed for an hour by thousands of reporters from all over the world. You get some questions about football, but with the NFL giving credentials to "reporters" from places such as Comedy Central, you also get a lot of crazy questions about all kinds of topics. You have men and women dressed in different costumes. One year, a woman actually showed up in a wedding dress to ask Tom Brady if he would marry her. I don't think his wife appreciated that one.

For Super Bowl 50, Media Night was in the SAP Center, better known as the Shark Tank, where the NHL's San Jose Sharks play. The Carolina Panthers went first. As we were standing backstage waiting to enter the arena, Aqib figured we should get in the spirit of the offbeat kind of questions we all knew we were going to hear at some point. He took off a giant gold chain he was wearing and put it around my neck. Then he grabbed a microphone from our team's camera crew and said, "Let me interview you, Coach."

"Okay, go ahead," I said.

"Coach, you're drippin' now. You're drippin'."

"Yeah, I'm drippin', baby. I'm really drippin'…What's 'drippin'?"

Aqib explained that it was a lyric from a song that talks about having all kinds of gold chains and stuff around your neck. We had a lot of fun with that. Those are the moments that make the Super Bowl experience special. It had been twenty-six years since the only other time I coached in a Super Bowl, also with the Broncos. You never know when you're going to be in another one, so you have to enjoy it while you can.

Almost every player that's been around me can tell you that I've said the same thing before every game: "I want you to go out and play as hard as you can play. We practiced everything we had to practice. Now, you go out and play as hard as you can play, every play, and don't look back. And any mistake you make is mine."

That way, the players can play without worrying about making mistakes.

The night before the Super Bowl, which was going to be played at Levi's Stadium in Santa Clara, I made a speech to the defense. I purposely didn't say anything about the mistakes, just to see if they were paying attention. I started to walk out of the room, and a bunch of the players said, "Coach, what about the mistakes?"

"Oh, yeah," I said with a smile. "The mistakes are mine."

They started laughing.

There's nothing like the electricity of the Super Bowl. The whole atmosphere is unlike anything you ever experience in football or sports or pretty much anything else for that matter. Everything is bigger than life.

We were standing there on the sidelines getting ready for the national anthem, which is special when you hear it before any game but has an extra special feel to it before the Super Bowl. Lady Gaga sang it. I'll admit I wasn't a big follower of hers before then. I didn't know much about her at all. It wasn't until after the game that my wife, Laurie, told me, "She's a really great singer, Wade." That was pretty easy to tell, because she belted out the national anthem about as close to the way Whitney Houston sang it before Super Bowl XXV as anybody has ever done. What I loved about Lady Gaga was that she wasn't flamboyant about it. I thought, *Wow! This gal can really sing.*

• • •

The main thing I had stressed to the players in our defensive meetings through the two weeks leading up to the game was that we wanted to stop the Panthers' running game. I wasn't just talking about their running backs. I was talking about their quarterback, Cam Newton, who finished the regular season as the top rushing quarterback in the NFL. I also pointed out that while the Panthers had a heck of an offense and were scoring thirty points a game, they were nineteenth in the league in passing.

"We've played a lot better passing teams than what they are," I said. "If we get them to pass the ball, then we have an advantage because of our pass rush. This is realistic."

A big part of our defensive plan was to put a "spy" on Newton. That meant one of our linebackers, Von Miller, was assigned to basically follow his every move. Wherever he went in the pocket, Von had to be right with him and ready to tackle him if he decided to run with the ball.

Early in the game, Newton scrambled a little bit, and we got the feeling that we could stop him and let our guys rush and make plays on him rather than letting him get out of the pocket and make plays that way. With Von spying and then having three other guys rush, we felt we were pretty well in control. We had someone accounting for Cam and we knew we could cover their receivers, who weren't as good as the receivers on the two previous teams we played, the Patriots and Steelers. The Panthers' passing game just wasn't as good as what the Patriots and Steelers had.

Going in, conventional thinking was: Don't let Newton run with it; make him throw the ball. And don't let the Panthers run the ball from their read option or just their normal running game, because Jonathan Stewart is a good back. The Panthers had made a lot of yardage and controlled games by running the football.

But at the start, we were giving Cam some time to throw. He didn't run with it, but we weren't getting enough pressure on him, so we decided to let our guys rush. We told them, "Don't let him get out of the pocket, but if you can put pressure on them, that's a better deal."

We went back to the stuff that we basically did against Tom Brady as far as rushing the passer. We used a four-man rush and they had some chip formations, where they chipped on the outside guys, using running backs and tight ends to help the tackles block before they ran their pass patterns. We knew when they were going to be doing that and we were ready with some things to combat it, like having some safeties rush Newton. That way, the Panthers' offensive linemen couldn't double-team anybody and the backs and tight ends couldn't chip block, because some-body was always running in there to get the quarterback.

They usually had two backs split in the backfield—although most of the time, one of them was the second tight end—and the quarterback was in shotgun formation right in between them. The two backs would step to the left and the whole line would go to the right, building a wall to protect Newton as he dropped back to pass.

It was a college protection, which we really don't see that much in the NFL. It also wasn't a very good protection and we took advantage of that by sending linebackers and safeties from the side opposite the way the offensive linemen were going. Sometimes, we had three rushers going against two blockers. Sometimes, they had five blockers against two rushers on the other side, but we made sure we kept someone outside to make sure Cam couldn't turn the corner.

Von Miller had a great game, with two-and-a-half sacks and two forced fumbles, and was voted Super Bowl MVP. Von played tremendously well in all three games of the postseason. I mean, he gets off the line so quick, a tackle can barely get out of his stance before Von's already going around him. We thought they'd chip him more than they did. They hardly chipped him at all.

Von has one of the best spin moves I've ever seen. That's hard to do for a lot of pass rushers. You have to have a really great center of gravity. When you spin, you've got to be able to spin forward. You can't spin in one place, like a top. We worked on that with him in practice, but we didn't work on it with other guys because they couldn't do it as well as him. One of the only other players in the same league as Von as far as spin moves is Dwight Freeney. But there haven't been a whole lot of other players with the balance and athleticism to be able to accelerate past the blocker after they spin.

DeMarcus Ware also played a good game, with two sacks. One of them came with eleven seconds left in the half and us holding a 13–7 lead. The Panthers didn't have any timeouts and they were going to throw the ball from our forty-five, trying to get in field goal range. DeMarcus hit him right in the back, killing the scoring opportunity, so we ended the half on a high note.

We went up 16–7 in the third quarter, but the Panthers cut it to 16–10 in the fourth. When we got the ball back with 7:07 left, I figured the offense would be pretty aggressive and try to score to put the game out of reach or at least extend the drive to run time off the clock. But on third and nine from the Denver twenty-six, we ran the ball. C. J. Anderson only picked up a couple of yards, and we were forced to punt it away with just under five minutes left.

I was thinking myself, *What are we doing? We're not even trying to make a first down?* I've always believed that, in a situation where you have to make a first down, you throw the ball. That's what professional football is. You've got to be able to throw the ball on third and seven or third and nine, and get the first down.

Gary Kubiak agrees with that philosophy. That's why he walked over to me on the sidelines and apologized for not throwing the ball.

"We had a pass play called," he said. "But Manning thought he saw a chance to get a nice gain on a run play, so he audibled to the run."

"That's okay," I said.

To a lot of people who didn't know that, it looked like we were just trying to let our defense win or lose the game. In other words, put it all on the defense. Even the TV commentators and other people in the media said, "That's a great strategy. The Broncos have got a great defense. That'll win you the game." Of course, that wasn't our strategy at all. Gary wanted to pick up the first down. Peyton did too. He thought he saw something in the Panthers' defense he could exploit, but it didn't work out.

Still, it did put the game on our defense, which was pretty much the case the whole season. We had a lot of those situations and responded well. I believe our defense played under pressure better than any team I've been around.

Von Miller is probably as good as anybody at playing under pressure. He made a lot of plays at the end of games. He sacked Tom Brady in overtime when we beat the Patriots in the regular season. He took the ball away from the Oakland quarterback, Derek Carr, late in a win against the Raiders. And Chris Harris intercepted a pass and returned it seventy-four yards to win that game. Aqib Talib intercepted a pass against Cleveland and returned it sixty-three yards for a touchdown. It was just went on and on like that. Our guys made plays when they were absolutely necessary. They didn't panic under pressure.

They also had a lot of confidence in themselves. They knew what they were doing. They didn't make many mental mistakes. We just had that kind of group.

• • •

The Panthers got the ball with 4:51 left. If they drove for a touchdown, they could have won the game. But Von sacked Cam and forced him to fumble. Cam didn't jump into the pile to go after the ball—which T. J. Ward recovered for us at the

Carolina four-yard line—and he took a lot of criticism for that. Some people were criticizing his toughness.

I don't know about that. Cam's pretty tough. He runs over guys to get into the end zone, so I don't think he was scared or anything. I just think he made a bad decision. I think he thought one of his teammates was going to get the ball. It was just one of those snap decisions, and he made the wrong one.

On third down, Peyton Manning threw an incomplete pass, but a defensive holding penalty put the ball at the two. C. J. Anderson ran for a touchdown and Peyton threw to Bennie Fowler for a two-point conversion to make it 24–10. That was the final score.

● ● ●

It took me thirty-eight years to be a part of a Super Bowl victory. You realize at the end of it that you're the best in the world. Nobody can deny that. When I talked to the 2016 team before the season, I said, "We want to be better in a lot of areas, but you can't get any better than winning the Super Bowl."

That goes for coaching, too. To be the best in the world at least once? I felt that, for sure. But it wasn't like I ever felt there was something lacking in my career because I didn't have a Super Bowl ring. My dad never talked about that, either. For one thing, he never looked back. NFL Films made a highlight film of his career. We had some great teams and great games during our years in Houston—even when we lost to Pittsburgh two years in a row in the AFC Championship Game—but no matter what happens with your team, the people who put those highlight films together always do a great job. You might win

only two games in a season and they'll make it look like you won thirty, like you won the Super Bowl.

During a family gathering after Daddy retired, my sisters and I said, "Dad, let's watch that Oilers highlight film."

"No, I don't want to watch that," he said. "We've already done that. I'm looking forward."

He never dwelled in the past—never reaching the Super Bowl didn't bother him. He felt he did the best he could do, just like the players and the rest of us on the coaching staff. If it worked out and we won the Super Bowl, great. If it didn't, he didn't have any regrets. He just went on to the next thing—whether it was a play or a series or a game or a season...or to his ranch. Whatever it was, he was moving on to it.

Coaches and players always like to say they don't read the paper or they don't listen to what other people say about them or their teams, but I do. What I don't do is look back and say, "Well, gosh, I wish we would have won the Super Bowl when we were 13–3 at Dallas and we had the last drive against the Giants and didn't score and they ended up beating us and winning the Super Bowl." Or the AFC Championship Games against Pittsburgh. Or even the '91 Denver team that could have easily gone to the Super Bowl but had a close loss to Buffalo for the conference title.

I'm just one of those people who are happy with what's happening in their life. You always want to do more. You always hope things get better. You do get personally upset when you hear people say, "He couldn't do this," or, "He didn't do that," or, "He didn't win here." And you say, "Well, yeah, that's true, but I can't do anything about it now."

That's just the way I think about it.

The Music City deal doesn't even bother me. Not anymore. I mean, we played the best we could. We almost beat a team that wound up losing in the Super Bowl. It's all ifs and buts and that kind of stuff, but we played pretty darned well and had our opportunities.

Now I'm part of a team that fulfilled the ultimate goal of winning the whole deal. It bonds the team forever, even though I stopped being a part of it after the 2016 season, when I became defensive coordinator for the Los Angeles Rams. Any reunion ten or fifteen years from now, we will be getting together as the Super Bowl 50-winning team. That's the neat thing about being part of this. The "Luv Ya Blue" Houston Oilers still get together. They didn't win it all, but they accomplished probably more than they should have and I've been to a lot of reunions with those guys through the years.

Unfortunately, they all got together at my dad's funeral, too. At the time, Wesley was still working for the Cowboys. The funeral was in Goliad. When Daddy passed away, I called Jerry Jones and told him and he said, "I'll send Wes and his family down there with my plane." Not only did he see to it

that Wes was able to attend the funeral, but he also made sure that his wife and our grandchildren were there too. People don't realize some of the things that Jerry does for people. I'll never forget that.

As the final seconds were ticking off the clock in the Super Bowl, Kub walked over, patted me on the head, and said, "Your dad would really be proud of you."

I kind of ducked my head, because it took my breath away. I really appreciated that he said that. I thought, *Yes, Daddy would be proud of me.* I was sixty-eight years old and I still wanted my dad to be proud of me. That's just the way I am. That's the way I've always been.

It all hit me in that moment, with all the confetti coming down, and especially when my family—Laurie and my son, Wesley, and my daughter, Tracy—came out onto the field with me. Being with them made me think about my father even more. It made it such an emotional moment.

Of course, he's always in my thoughts, which was something I shared with our guys on defense during the 2015 season. Each year I always tell players that they need to dedicate a game to somebody other than themselves. I do the same thing myself from time to time. I think you need to be reminded every once in a while that it's not all about you. There's somebody else in your life that's probably meant a lot to you besides your teammates and coaches and anyone else directly connected to the team.

On October 4, 2015, the Broncos were going to face the Minnesota Vikings. I picked that game as the one I wanted to dedicate to my father, because it was a home game closest to the date that he died, October 18, 2013. During our defensive meeting the night before the game, I said, "You don't just play for yourself. You play for your teammates; you play for other people with the team. And every once in a while, you ought to dedicate a game to someone special. It could be your granddad, it could be your grandmother who raised you, whoever. This game is close to the date when my dad passed away, and I'm going to dedicate my coaching in this game to him."

We won 23–20. It was our fourth victory on the way to a 7–0 start. With about thirty seconds left, T. J. Ward forced the Vikings' quarterback, Teddy Bridgewater, to fumble and Von recovered to ice the game for us. The next morning we had our usual meeting as a defense before breaking into position groups to watch film. I usually start off by pointing out the goals we met during the game, but before I could say anything, one of the defensive backs said, "Coach, we've got something for you." He handed me a ball, signed by every member of the defense.

"This is for you and your dad," he said.

I've gotten many game balls in my career that were given out by the head coach. I've gotten them for when our defense had a great game. I've gotten them for being a part of division and conference championships. But I had never received one from the entire defense. That meant so much to me. I think it meant something to the players, too. It was just a special moment and I broke down in front of everybody in our meeting room. I saw it as a bonding experience. I won't speak for them, but I know it was for me.

I know Daddy would have been excited about what was taking place in my career. After he retired, he did some radio announcing with the Oilers, but he was mostly living football through me. He didn't come to the games, because he wanted to watch them on TV where he could run the plays back and forth on his recorder. We talked after every game and he would tell me what I should and shouldn't have done.

To this day, I still can hear his voice. I still can feel his presence. I still can see him wearing his ten-gallon hat and cowboy boots.

As blessed as I am to have gotten that first Super Bowl ring, I'm even more blessed that I got to spend all of those years coaching with my dad.

ACKNOWLEDGMENTS

THE AUTHORS WISH TO THANK, IN ALPHABETICAL ORDER, THE following for their contributions to this book: Will Bennett, for his superb editing; Lindsay Gorman, for being an extra set of eyes and hands throughout; Jaime Levine, for her wonderful big-picture vision and guidance every step of the way; Taylor Ness, for taking care of the details; Gary O'Hagan, for seeing a tremendous idea for a book and working so diligently to make it happen; and last but certainly not least, Scott Waxman, for recognizing that this father-son story needed to be told and that Diversion would do the best job of helping us tell it.

WADE PHILLIPS IS AN INNOVATIVE CHAMPION FOOTBALL COACH with a long career in the NFL. Considered the best defensive coordinator in the league, he helped the Denver Broncos win the Super Bowl in 2016. Smothering and punishing, Wade's Denver defense was favorably compared with some of the best of all time. In thirty-four seasons as a coordinator or a head coach, Wade's defenses have finished top ten in the NFL in twenty-four of them. No wonder he was voted NFL's 2015 Assistant Coach of the Year by the Associated Press. In January, 2017, he became the defensive coordinator for the Los Angeles Rams.

VIC CARUCCI HAS COVERED THE NFL AS A WRITER AND BROAD-caster for thirty-seven years. Vic covers the NFL for the *Buffalo News* and is a regular cohost for SiriusXM NFL Radio. He is a former columnist for NFL.com and NFL Network contributor. He has received multiple honors from the Associated Press and the Pro Football Writers of America. He is the author of nine previous books about pro football.